PRAISE FOR *SAVED AS THROUGH FIRE*

"How do imperfect human beings arrive in heaven? How are they changed by God after death to prepare them for beatitude? To grapple with the mystery we call purgatory is to think more deeply about our common human condition, as we are all confronted with death and the afterlife. The Church's teaching on purgatory is filled with hope and consolation. In this book Fr. Luke Wilgenbusch provides us with a wonderful theological introduction to Aquinas's teaching on purgatory, illustrates its genuine insight, and shows us its ecumenical promise. This book provides a standard reference for those seeking greater understanding of the Church's teaching on life after death."

Thomas Joseph White, O.P.
Pontifical University of Saint Thomas Aquinas

———————•———————

"Sadly, and much to the detriment of Church life, the doctrines of purgatory and indulgences have been often ridiculed for their apparent theological inconsistencies. In truth, the full remission of temporal punishment is a revelation of the perfection and love of God—and the depths to which he redeems the fallen human race not only from the guilt of sin but also the disorders that sin causes. In *Saved as through Fire*, Fr. Wilgenbusch gives a treatment of the full scope of salvation in Christ—salvation that makes it possible for the redeemed to love God with rectitude for all eternity. This book thus demonstrates with much needed lucidity that the Catholic teaching on the remission of the temporal consequences of sin is not a human construct but the logical consequence of the realization of God's eternal plan to restore all things in Christ. By means of the outstanding scholarship and careful thinking that are evidenced on every page of this volume, readers will come away with an inspiring understanding of who they are destined to be for all eternity as a result of the transformative impact of the grace of God merited for them by Jesus Christ."

Roger W. Nutt
Ave Maria University

———————•———————

"Purgatory has fallen off the radar of many Catholics, but it has become a fruitful point of engagement between Catholic, Protestant, and Orthodox theologians. Fr. Luke Wilgenbusch opens up the theology of purgatory in this clear and comprehensive analysis, showing both its importance for Christian hope and its ecumenical potential."

Michael Root
Catholic University of America

———————•———————

"If there is anything more misunderstood than the Church's traditional understanding of purgatory among contemporary Christians, both Protestant and Catholic, I have yet to find it. Readers will find in this volume a comprehensive, extremely detailed and workman-like treatment of all the basic issues surrounding the Church's traditional teaching about purgatory, punishment, and satisfaction. Whether one agrees or disagrees with the Catholic Church's traditional teaching about purgatory, one can find here all the basic texts and responses to all the major objections. Hence this book will likely remain an essential resource for anyone interested in these questions for years to come."

Randall B. Smith
University of St. Thomas

RENEWAL WITHIN TRADITION

SERIES EDITOR: MATTHEW LEVERING

Matthew Levering is the James N. and Mary D. Perry Jr. Chair of Theology at Mundelein Seminary. Levering is the author or editor of over thirty books. He serves as coeditor of the journals *Nova et Vetera* and the *International Journal of Systematic Theology*.

ABOUT THE SERIES

Catholic theology reflects upon the content of divine revelation as interpreted and handed down in the Church, but today Catholic theologians often find the scriptural and dogmatic past to be alien territory. The Renewal within Tradition Series undertakes to reform and reinvigorate contemporary theology from within the tradition, with St. Thomas Aquinas as a central exemplar. As part of its purpose, the series reunites the streams of Catholic theology that, prior to the Council, separated into neo-scholastic and *nouvelle theologie* modes. The biblical, historical-critical, patristic, liturgical, and ecumenical emphases of the Ressourcement movement need the dogmatic, philosophical, scientific, and traditioned enquiries of Thomism, and vice versa. Renewal within Tradition challenges the regnant forms of theological liberalism that, by dissolving the cognitive content of the gospel, impede believers from knowing the love of Christ.

PUBLISHED OR FORTHCOMING

Reading the Sermons of Thomas Aquinas: A Beginner's Guide
Randall B. Smith

The Culture of the Incarnation: Essays in Catholic Theology
Tracey Rowland

Self-Gift: Humanae Vitae and the Thought of John Paul II
Janet E. Smith

On Love and Virtue: Theological Essays
Michael S. Sherwin, O.P.

Aquinas on Beatific Charity and the Problem of Love
Christopher J. Malloy

SAVED AS
THROUGH FIRE

SAVED AS THROUGH FIRE

---•---

A Thomistic Account of Purgatory, Temporal Punishment, and Satisfaction

LUKE WILGENBUSCH

EMMAUS
ACADEMIC

Steubenville, Ohio
www.emmausacademic.com

EMMAUS
ACADEMIC

Steubenville, Ohio
A Division of The St. Paul Center for Biblical Theology
Editor-in-Chief: Scott Hahn
1468 Parkview Circle
Steubenville, Ohio 43952

Library of Congress Cataloging-in-Publication Data
Names: Wilgenbusch, Luke, author.
Title: Saved as through fire : a Thomistic account of purgatory, temporal punishment, and satisfaction / Luke
  Wilgenbusch.
Description: Steubenville, Ohio : Emmaus Academic, 2023. | Series: Renewal within tradition | Expansion of the
  author's thesis (doctoral)--Pontifical University of St. Thomas Aquinas, 2020, under the title: Saved through
  fire : a Thomistic account of purgatory. | Includes bibliographical references and index. | Summary: "In contem-
  porary considerations of purgatory, there is increasing ecumenical agreement among Catholics, Orthodox, and
  Protestants about the need for spiritual purification and healing before a soul can enter into the glory of God's
  presence in heaven. Yet for the broader tradition of the Church, this account of what souls require from God is
  paired with a complementary account of what God, in his justice, requires of the soul, including satisfaction of its
  "debt of punishment" (reatus poenae). Although the transformative and retributive aspects of purgatory are often
  seen today as being at odds with one another, Fr. Luke Wilgenbusch proposes in Saved as through Fire to recover
  their proper and traditional harmony. Taking Thomas Aquinas as his primary guide, Wilgenbusch identifies and
  explores the full array of the consequences of sin-both immanent and extrinsic-that purgatory resolves. Through
  an attentive retrieval of Aquinas's teaching on sin, its effects, and its remedy in Christ, Wilgenbusch clarifies how
  purgatory indeed heals and purifies souls from their guilt and disordered attachments, and how it simultaneously
  serves as a form of punishment and a means of satisfaction, enabling souls to contribute, in union with Christ,
  to the restoration of the divine order of creation damaged by their sin. Beyond shedding valuable light on the
  doctrine of purgatory, the integrated vantage on purification, punishment, and satisfaction provided by Saved as
  through Fire holds promise, too, for a better understanding of the Church's practices of penance, reparation, and
  the offering of indulgences"-- Provided by publisher.
Identifiers: LCCN 2023051333 (print) | LCCN 2023051334 (ebook) | ISBN 9781645853350 (hardcover) | ISBN
  9781645853367 (paperback) | ISBN 9781645853374 (ebook)
Subjects: LCSH: Purgatory--History of doctrines. | Sin--Christianity--History of doctrines. | Salvation--
  Christianity--History of doctrines. | Thomas, Aquinas, Saint, 1225?-1274.
Classification: LCC BT843 .W55 2023 (print) | LCC BT843 (ebook) | DDC
  236/.5--dc23/eng/20231130
LC record available at https://lccn.loc.gov/2023051333
LC ebook record available at https://lccn.loc.gov/2023051334

Nihil Obstat	*Imprimatur*
Very Reverend John J. H. Hammond, V.G., J.C.L.	Most Reverend J. Mark Spalding, D.D., L.C.L.
Censor Librorum	Bishop of Nashville
	January 24, 2023

Cover design and layout by Allison Merrick.
Cover image *Holy Souls in Purgatory* mural, St. Casimir Church, Baltimore. Photo credit: Fr. James Bradley.

To Mom and Dad:
Thank you for all of your love, prayers, and encouragement!

Thus wrongdoing is second of evils in greatness; but to do wrong and not pay the penalty is the greatest and takes the first place among all evils.

PLATO, GORGIAS

Ah! in what a monstrous moment of pride and passion he had prayed that the portrait should bear the burden of his days, and he keep the unsullied splendour of eternal youth! All his failure had been due to that. Better for him that each sin of his life had brought its sure swift penalty along with it. There was purification in punishment. Not "Forgive us our sins" but "Smite us for our iniquities" should be the prayer of man to a most just God.

OSCAR WILDE, THE PICTURE OF DORIAN GRAY

Table of Contents

Introduction

IN A 2015 SYMPOSIUM HOSTED by the Apostolic Penitentiary, Archbishop Rino Fisichella, the president of the Pontifical Council for the Promotion of the New Evangelization, delivered a short paper entitled "Le indulgenze: definizione della problematica."[1] In the conclusion he highlighted a few open questions in the field for contemporary theology. In particular, he noted the need for a re-elaboration of the sense of the *reatus poenae* in light of modern anthropology.[2] Traditionally, the term *reatus poenae* refers to the debt of punishment that man owes to divine justice for his sins. Admittedly, such a notion is not so easily accepted or understood today and often carries many unpleasant connotations that harken back to the brutality of prior ages. One cannot help but imagine the "pound of flesh" mercilessly demanded by Shylock in Shakespeare's *Merchant of Venice*. Nevertheless, as Fisichella's paper recognizes, the proper understanding of divine punishment is unavoidable for the theology of indulgences and therefore of purgatory as well.

While sharing Fisichella's concern to present this doctrine in a way that is accessible in our contemporary context, I would argue that what is first needed is a proper understanding of the term's original meaning. Certainly, there is space for doctrinal development, but there is also a great risk in all too quickly "updating" the language of previous generations when the truths of divine revelation are at stake. Did the theologians of the past really believe that God punishes the souls of the just as they undergo purification? What sense or purpose could punishment have for those who are already in friendship with God? A robust theology of purgatory will have to address these issues.

---

[1] Rino Fisichella, "Le indulgenze: definizione della problematica," (Rome: Apostolic Penitentiary, 2015), accessed April 3, 2010, http://www.penitenzieria.va/content/dam/penitenzieriaapostolica/indulgenze/Fisichella.pdf.

[2] Fisichella, "Le indulgenze," 11.

1

Additionally, many today speak about purgatory primarily in terms of the soul's interior transformation. Purgatory is, after all, a time of healing. The common imagination and popular catechesis tend to prefer this mode of presentation. It is felt to be more in keeping with the dignity of the human person and his authentic freedom. In this description God's love and mercy are more easily discernable. Nevertheless, although there are clear precedents for this perspective in the tradition (e.g., Dante's *Divine Comedy*), one cannot help but suspect that this is not the primary meaning of the pain of purgatory, traditionally referred to as "temporal punishment." Any account of punishment has to be significantly reworked and nuanced in order to avoid the unpleasant connotations of divine retribution. If painful transformation was all that was intended by the classical terminology, any number of more obvious descriptions might have been chosen. Nevertheless, despite the tension, the popular intuition about the need for transformation after death consistently perdures.

In these two frames, then—punishment and healing—the heart of the question of purgatory comes to the fore. What does it mean to be completely purified and prepared for heaven? What is the relationship between justice and moral transformation? Is the punishment of purgatory medicinal or purely retributive? For the purposes of this book, I will follow the thought of St. Thomas Aquinas on these questions. His theology has proved to be an abundant source of wisdom and understanding for the Church throughout the centuries.

Before presenting the outline of the work, however, it will be helpful to lay out some conceptual and terminological clarifications. These distinctions will be more clearly outlined in the chapters that follow, but it is beneficial to have the basic framework in mind from the start. First, sin is an action and hence has no continued existence after its performance. In a proper technical sense, one cannot say, for instance, that sin is *in* someone except when he is in the act of sinning. Rather, what remains with the subject are the consequences of sin: the *reatus culpae* (guilt), the *reatus poenae* (debt of punishment), the habitual weakening of the faculties ("evil dispositions"), and self-imposed consequences, even if involuntary (remorse, grief, etc.).

Reatus culpae is the primary intrinsic consequence of sin and can be translated as "debt of guilt." It is also often referred to simply as "guilt" (in the juridical sense, as distinct from the emotional experience of remorse consequent upon the judgment of conscience). This *reatus culpae* is a disordering of the actual will away from God, and it is overcome when man's will is reordered to God through the working of supernatural charity. The change within the subject is "contrition," and the consequent restoration of friendship with God is called "forgiveness." Throughout this book I will typically refer to the *reatus culpae* as "guilt." However, Aquinas regularly interchanges "sin" and "guilt" in this context, and I will also alternate between the two for rhetorical ease, recognizing, nevertheless, that "guilt" is technically the more proper term.

Reatus poenae is the primary extrinsic consequence of sin and is usually translated as "debt of punishment." This term, as we will see in much more detail, refers to a man's indebtedness to divine justice after having committed a sin. For reasons I will show, the sinner must suffer an adequate punishment before God for his fault. The debt of punishment is resolved when justice is restored through the undergoing of a sufficient punishment.

"Punishment," likewise, is a complex term of central importance for this book. I will use "punishment," from the Latin *poena*, in the widest possible sense (and not as we typically do in English) to refer to anything that the rational creature suffers against his will. Someone is punished when this evil is imposed upon him from outside. In distinction, punishment is called "satisfaction" when that which is against one's will is voluntarily accepted as a means for restoring justice.[3] Satisfaction thus falls within the genus of punishment, broadly speaking. At times throughout the book, I will also use "atoning" or "making reparation" as synonyms for "making satisfaction," for the sake of rhetorical variety.

Finally, in addition to the *reatus culpae* and *reatus poenae*, there are also secondary consequences of sin in the soul of the individual. These can be divided between the automatic consequences that I will typically refer to as "evil dispositions" and the self-imposed consequences that result from conscience's judgment of one's moral failure, such as remorse. Like the *reatus culpae* these consequences reside in the soul of the sinner, and yet like the *reatus poenae* they are a kind of punishment. As distinct from divine punishments, however, these consequences can be called punishments of the order of reason since they flow directly from nature and from man's own conscience. Throughout the book I commonly refer to the overcoming of the evil dispositions as "(moral) transformation" or "healing."

There are a few different ways that these categories can be grouped. What I have called the primary consequences, *reatus culpae* and *reatus poenae*, deal directly with God and can be linked together according to that criterion. *Reatus culpae* is the most directly tied to the action of sin itself

---

[3] For some recent literature on debates around satisfaction, see Benedict M. Guevin, "Anselm and Aquinas on Satisfaction," *Angelicum* 87 (2010): 283–90; and Jerry Bracken, "Thomas Aquinas and Anselm's Satisfaction Theory," *Angelicum* 62 (1985): 501–30.

since it is the direct and immediate result in the will itself, the faculty at the root of all sin. For this reason, guilt is often in a category of its own and is simply called "sin," as we saw above. When seen from this perspective, the *reatus poenae*, evil dispositions, and feelings of remorse can be collectively referred to as the "consequences of sin" or even as "imperfections." Further, when the punishment of hell is excluded, the three consequences of sin can be referred to as "temporal punishment." At other times, given the primacy of divine matters, temporal punishment refers exclusively to the non-eternal punishments directed specifically to the *reatus poenae*. This variation in terminology can cause misunderstandings and is part of the reason for confusion on this topic. Nevertheless, with these important clarifications it is typically possible to discern which distinctions are being emphasized in any presentation.

Regarding sources, it must be noted that Aquinas does not have a complete systematic treatise on purgatory. The topic only appears occasionally in the disputed questions, and Aquinas did not reach this theme before abruptly terminating his *Summa theologiae*. In other words, there is no single source sufficient for articulating a Thomistic account of purgatory. The main text will be his commentary on the *Sentences*, but this early work contains many elements that were better developed and explained at other places in Aquinas's mature corpus. Thus, a certain amount of combination and synthesis will be required. Similarly, there is a lamentable dearth of contemporary secondary material on the topic from a Thomistic perspective. Charles Journet's 1966 article on indulgences and Phillipe-Marie Margelidon's 2016 development of the former are notable exceptions.[4]

That being said, I believe that a genuine Thomistic account of purgatory can still be discovered. In the first chapter of this book I will use Aquinas's anthropology to identify the relevant objects of purification. We will see that there are three obstacles to the beatific vision that remain after death: the guilt of venial sins not yet forgiven (*reatus culpae*), residual evil dispositions, and the debt of punishment (*reatus poenae*). In chapter two I will survey significant theologians who have argued against one of these objects. I will give particular attention to the debates between Catholics and the Orthodox and Protestants. From this perspective it will already become clear that punishment and the *reatus poenae* is the central concept for the proper understanding of purgatory. Thus, in chapter three, I will present Aquinas's

---

[4]   Charles Journet, "Théologie des indulgences," *Nova et Vetera* 41, no. 2 (1966): 81–111; Philippe-Marie Margelidon, "Le Peines Purificatrices: Thomas D'Aquin et Charles Journet, et la Question Œcumenique du Purgatoire," *Bulletin de Littérature Ecclésiastique* 117, no. 1 (2016), 69–94.

punitive theory as a way to understand the true role and nature of punishment for sin. In this sense, although I will not say very much there about
purgatory directly, this chapter will be the most essential for understanding
Aquinas's explanation of the fundamental raison d'être of purgatory. He, like
nearly all other Catholic theologians throughout the centuries, understood
purgatory as a primarily punitive experience.

Having said that, it is also my claim in this book that Aquinas's principles
can similarly be used to account for the transformative dimension of purgatory, the overcoming of the evil dispositions. I maintain a certain reserve
about judging what Aquinas himself thought. I do not think he provides
us enough evidence to allow us to know with certainty. Nevertheless, it is
a fair and reasonable adaptation of his thought to incorporate a notion of
medicinal punishment in purgatory. In chapter four, therefore, I will show
how I believe this can be done. In short, the divine illumination of the soul
that accompanies its separated state might be providentially directed to
produce a deep sorrow for past sins (punishment) that brings about any
final needed rectification of the will through repeated acts of love (healing).
When properly understood, this account of medicinal punishment balances
the real and sober demands of divine justice with the progressive healing
that so many find intuitively reasonable.

Finally, after having presented this account of purgatory, in the last two
chapters I will describe how this understanding relates to satisfactory works
and indulgences. By recourse to these means, man can do much to mitigate,
if not even eliminate, the need for purgatory, both for himself and those for
whom he prays. As the previous chapters will have shown, the debt of punishment is the primary obstacle that causes the souls of the faithful departed
to be delayed in purgatory. There are, nevertheless, many opportunities to
eliminate that debt, even while alive. Chief among these, as we will see, are
indulgences. By these gracious concessions the Church authoritatively applies
to the faithful the surplus treasury of satisfaction left to her by Christ and
the saints. In so doing, she greatly alleviates their burdens and encourages
them to grow in charity by performing works of piety and devotion. In this
way, when souls are earnest in their commitment to divine justice, they also
grow in deeper friendship with God. The dynamic interplay between the
medicinal and punitive elements of divine punishment is, therefore, only
amplified when satisfaction is undertaken on earth. While still living, the
soul can merit an increase in charity, which is of much greater value than the
mere remission of temporal punishment, important though the latter may be.

It is my hope that this account of purgatory and satisfaction brings
greater clarity to a topic that has become obscured or forgotten for many

today. Once again, we will see that the angelic doctor has much to offer contemporary theology. Rather than simply being a monument of an earlier age, his theological insight offers a valuable resource today for navigating the complex relationship between competing perspectives. His conceptual rigor is both stable enough to ensure continuity with the tradition of the Church and clear enough to incorporate subsequent developments. In just this way, he provided the essential tools for the simultaneously punitive and medicinal purgatory that I present in this book. It is my firm conviction that more theological fruit will be reaped the more his thought is engaged in the contemporary context.

CHAPTER I

Obstacles to the Beatific Vision in Purgatory

AT THE BEGINNING OF THIS Thomistic account of purgatory it is important to lay out the basic presuppositions behind such a work. There are many relevant doctrines which Aquinas both maintains and defends but that must be presumed here, at least at the beginning. I will explain and defend some of these ideas in more detail in chapter four, but for now we must simply accept them. At the most basic level Aquinas argues, both from reason and from faith, in favor of the existence of an immaterial, immortal soul.[1] Following Aristotle, he teaches that the soul is distinct from the body but is the form of the body. Hence, its natural state is to be incarnate, and accordingly, although it survives the death of the body, its activity is severely limited after death.[2] It cannot perform its ordinary functions in the same way, and it is fixed immutably in the good that was pursued as its final end at the moment of death. Thus, there can be no formal change in its moral orientation for or against God, we might say, in the most generic terms. In accordance with this basic orientation, at the moment of death there is a particular judgment wherein the eternal fate of the soul is decided—either with God in heaven or without him in hell.[3] However, Aquinas believes, in accord with the Catholic tradition, that some souls destined for heaven are delayed in purgatory, which is distinct from hell.[4]

---

[1] Thomas Aquinas, *Summa Theologiae*, trans. Laurence Shapcote, ed. and rev. the Aquinas Institute (Green Bay, WI: The Aquinas Institute, 2018), Ia, q. 75 (hereafter, *ST*).

[2] *ST* Ia, q. 89.

[3] Thomas Aquinas, *Commentary on the Sentences of Peter Lombard: Book IV, Distinctions 1–13*, trans. Beth Mortensen (Green Bay, WI: The Aquinas Institute, 2018), bk. 4, dist. 47, q. 1, a. 1, qc. 1, ad 1 (hereafter, *Super Sent.*).

[4] *Super Sent.*, lib. 4, dist. 21, q.1.

It is the consistent teaching of the western Church, even from before the time of Aquinas, that the souls in purgatory had died in the love of God, and it is for this reason that they are often called the "holy souls." They possess charity and at their particular judgment were assured of their eternal salvation.[5] Since after this earthly life the time of merit and demerit has ended,[6] there can be no change to their essential reward or punishment even in this intermediate state. As I explained, they no longer have the ability to change their basic moral orientation. There remains no doubt, then, that they will dwell with God for all eternity in perfect beatitude. Nevertheless, they are not currently enjoying this eternal bliss; a period of intense suffering intervenes. Due to their charity, they are destined for the beatific vision, but obstacles still remain. Speaking about the celestial city of Jerusalem, the book of Revelation teaches that "nothing unclean shall enter,"[7] and Aquinas explains that "no one is admitted to the possession of eternal life unless he is free from all sin and imperfection."[8] These souls still await the beatific vision because some obstacle intervenes. Before their consummation in glory, then, these souls must undergo a purification to rid themselves of whatever inhibits their full possession of beatitude. Thus, in order to understand the nature of purgatory, we must first distinguish what possible sins and imperfections might remain in these holy souls. In the course of this chapter I will survey the possibilities with the help of Aquinas's anthropology. We will examine sin and its consequences in the human soul and in doing so will find that there are three objects which can remain to be purified in the separated soul: guilt for venial sins not yet forgiven (*reatus culpae*), remaining evil dispositions, and a debt of temporal punishment before divine justice (*reatus poenae*). It is for these three reasons that some holy souls are delayed in their possession of full beatitude.

---

5   Thomas Aquinas, *Summa contra Gentiles*, books III–IV, trans. Laurence Shapcote, ed. and rev. the Aquinas Institute (Green Bay, WI: The Aquinas Institute, 2019), bk. 4, cap. 91 (hereafter, *SCG*). Cf. Heinrich Denzinger, *Enchiridion symbolorum definitionum et declarationum de rebus fidei et morum: Compendium of Creeds, Definitions and Declarations on Matters of Faith and Morals,* ed. Peter Hünermann, Robert Fastiggi, and Anne Englund Nash, 43rd ed. (San Francisco: Ignatius Press, 2012), §1488 (hereafter, *Compendium*).

6   *SCG* IV, cap. 91.

7   Rev 21:27.

8   Thomas Aquinas, *Compendium Theologiae*, in *Opuscula 1: Treatises*, trans. Cyril Vollert, ed. and rev. the Aquinas Institute (Green Bay, Wisconsin: The Aquinas Institute, 2018), lib. 1, cap. 182: "quia ad vitam aeternam consequendam non perducitur nisi qui ab omni peccato et defectu fuerit immunis." All Latin texts of Aquinas are taken from Corpus Thomisticum, https://www.corpusthomisticum.org/.

SINS

According to the traditional teaching of the Catholic Church, which bases itself on Scripture, human beings who die in a state of grace no longer remain guilty of any mortal sins. Although they may have committed serious sins during their lifetime, they have been restored to the state of grace prior to death and the particular judgment by God. Aquinas and the Catholic tradition more generally presuppose that the guilt of mortal sin is fundamentally incompatible with charity, and charity is that which makes one worthy of eternal life.[9] Thus, it is clear that the souls in purgatory, having died in the love of God, do not still bear the guilt of mortal sin. As Aquinas explains, "for mortal sin, which is the contrary of charity, a person is eternally excluded from the society of the saints and eternal punishment is imposed."[10] This, of course, is nothing other than the pain of hell, which is the just consequence of having separated oneself from God in such a definitive way.

Venial Sins

On the other hand, it is possible for a soul to die with charity and yet still retain some unforgiven venial sins. An exposition of the nature of sin is necessary in order to bring this point fully to light. To begin, sin is any inordinate voluntary act.[11] According to the classic definition, it is "a word, deed, or desire contrary to the eternal law."[12] In an anthropological sense, it is an act which leads man away from his proper end. In a theological sense, it is an act which deviates from God's divine plan for man. These two perspectives, though distinct, are harmonious. Following God's law only ever leads to authentic human flourishing. In the ultimate analysis, God himself is man's true end, and no created good will ever satisfy man, even on a natural level.[13] Sin, therefore, can also be described as a turning away from God and a turning toward a creature—*aversio a Deo et conversio ad creaturam.*[14] It means placing something other than God, one's pride or health, for example, as one's final end and goal. When this basic reorientation of one's life is both conscious and deliberate concerning a grave matter, the sin is mortal.[15] In this

---

[9] *ST* IIa-IIae, q. 24, a. 12.

[10] *Super Sent.*, lib. 4, dist. 46, q. 1, a. 3: "pro peccato mortali, quod est contrarium caritati, aliquis in aeternum a societate sanctorum exclusus aeternae poenae."

[11] *ST* Ia-IIae, q. 71, a. 1.

[12] *ST* Ia-IIae, q. 71, a. 6: "peccatum est dictum vel factum vel concupitum contra legem aeternam."

[13] *ST* Ia-IIae, q. 2, a. 7.

[14] *ST* IIIa, q. 86, a. 4.

[15] *ST* Ia-IIae, q. 88.

case, forgiveness of the sin requires a new gratuitous gift of grace by which the sinner is able to redirect his life to God.[16] It is the infusion of charity and consequent repentance that undoes the *aversio a Deo* of his previous sin. This is the reason why there is such a fundamental incompatibility between charity and mortal sin, as I indicated above. Charity directs one's whole life toward God. Mortal sin directs it toward any other good.

Nevertheless, there is not this same radical opposition between charity and venial sin. One can continue in charity while committing venial sins. With these lighter sins, only the *conversio ad creaturam* is present.[17] Although in some sense the *aversio* is still active, it is imperfect and does not effect a true reorientation of one's life. The real fault of venial sin is an inordinate use of means to the end rather than a change in the end itself.[18] It is a detour, not a change in destination. As Aquinas explains, venial sin does not consist in acting *against* (*contra*) the law but *beside* (*praeter*) it.[19] For this reason, charity, the supernatural ordering of one's life to God, remains, and thus there is no apparent contradiction in the possibility of the guilt of venial sin remaining in the souls of the just, even after death.

At the same time, it is important to remember that thanks to God's great mercy, it is relatively easy to receive forgiveness for sins in this life. The charity still present in the soul, in the case of merely venial sins, for example, already carries within it the intrinsic possibility of forgiveness. No new outpouring of grace is necessary for the rectification of the soul in its moment of disorder.[20] All that is truly necessary is a movement of interior penance made possible by the habitual charity that the person already possesses.[21] In the life of a person habitually living in a state of grace, one can hope that this is happening with some regularity. At any moment the soul in possession of charity can act in accordance with that grace, make a genuine act of contrition, and thereby be forgiven. From this perspective it is not so obvious why venial sin would remain after death. In particular, one might imagine that the existential experience of death would occasion such a movement in an even more profound way. Aquinas himself was aware of this kind of objection. He writes that "some people have said that . . . the final

---

[16] *ST* Ia-IIae, q. 87, a. 3.

[17] *ST* Ia-IIae, q. 87, a. 5, ad 1. Réginald Garrigou-Lagrange, O.P., *Life Everlasting and the Immensity of the Soul*, trans. Patrick Cummins, O.S.B. (Rockford, IL: Tan Books, 1991), 173.

[18] *ST* Ia-IIae, q. 88, a. 1.

[19] *ST* Ia-IIae, q. 88, a. 1.

[20] *ST* IIIa, q. 87, a. 2.

[21] *ST* IIIa, q. 87, a. 2.

grace itself purifies from venial fault."[22] However, although there may often be such an opportunity at the moment of death, venial sin "is not remitted without an actual movement of contrition."[23] In other words, there must be a specific act accompanying that moment. The habitual intention consequent with charity, though a sufficient foundation for forgiveness, is not enough.

This point correlates with an interesting difference between venial and mortal sins. The infusion of the habit of charity is sufficient for the forgiveness of mortal sins because it is directly contrary to them. Mortal sins are all united in their definitive turn from God. Hence, if any one mortal sin is to be forgiven, they must all be forgiven by a genuine return to God in sanctifying grace.[24] Between having God or a created good as one's final end, there is no via media. However, because venial sins do not have the same formal unity, it is possible for some to be forgiven without others. John Joseph O'Brien explains, "Unlike mortal sins which have an internal nexus in their common aversion from God and destruction of the principle of charity, [venial sins] have no inner bond. So one can be remitted while others are not."[25] The habit of charity alone does not suffice for the forgiveness of these sins as it does for mortal sins. Hence, we see yet again that a specific act is required. The forgiveness of particular venial sins comes about only through an act of fervor in the charity already possessed habitually.[26]

Aquinas rightly points out that this movement of contrition does not always occur. He writes, "it can happen that after someone has committed a venial sin, he will not actually think anything about abandoning the sin or holding to it, but he thinks perhaps that a triangle has three angles equal to two right angles; and in this thought he falls asleep and dies."[27] Obviously, according to Aquinas's argument, this geometer has not yet been forgiven for his sin. The guilt remains. Nevertheless, because he maintained the love of God, he would ultimately still be destined for the beatific vision. His unforgiven venial sin does not destroy the charity based on which he would be judged worthy of heaven. However, the sin would still need to be

---

[22] *Super Sent.,* lib. 4, dist. 21, q. 1, a. 3, qc. 1: "quidam dixerunt . . . quia ipsa gratia finalis culpam purgat venialem."

[23] *Super Sent.,* lib. 4, dist. 21, q. 1, a. 3, qc. 1: "non dimittitur sine actuali contritionis motu."

[24] John Joseph O'Brien, "The Remission of Venial Sin" (STD diss., Catholic University of America, 1959), 52.

[25] O'Brien, "Remission of Venial Sin," 52.

[26] O'Brien, "Remission of Venial Sin," 51.

[27] *Super Sent.,* lib. 4, dist. 21, q. 1, a. 3, qc. 1: "Potest autem contingere quod aliquis postquam veniale peccatum commisit, nihil actualiter cogitet de peccato vel dimittendo vel tenendo; sed cogitet forte quod triangulus habet tres angulos aequales duobus rectis; et in hac cogitatione obdormiat, et moriatur."

remitted before he could receive his reward, for, as O'Brien notes, "the soul cannot enter heaven as long as it retains the guilt of sin."[28]

Aquinas joins a well-established school of biblical interpretation when he sees affirmation of this idea in our Lord's words in the twelfth chapter of Matthew.[29] There Jesus says, "And whoever says a word against the Son of man will be forgiven; but whoever speaks against the Holy Spirit will not be forgiven, either in this age *or in the age to come*."[30] Although he is speaking negatively—it will not be forgiven in the age to come—Jesus seems to suggest that some sins will be forgiven in that future state. As Gregory the Great aptly explained long before Aquinas:

> From this statement we learn that some sins can be forgiven in this world and some in the world to come. For, if forgiveness is refused for a particular sin, we conclude logically that it is granted for others. This must apply, as I said, to slight transgressions, such as persistent idle talking, immoderate laughter, or blame in the care of property . . . All these faults are troublesome for the soul after death if they are not forgiven while one is still alive.[31]

In this way, then, some venial sins not yet forgiven do constitute one of the obstacles to the holy soul's eternal reward that must be addressed in purgatory.

IMPERFECTIONS

The category of imperfection which follows is much broader than that of sin and will require a more detailed analysis. The first thing that can be said to orient the discussion is that this category can be loosely referred to

---

[28] O'Brien, "Remission of Venial Sin," 52.

[29] Thomas Aquinas, *Commentary on the Gospel of Matthew*, trans. Jeremy Holmes and Beth Mortensen, ed. the Aquinas Institute (Lander, WY: The Aquinas Institute, 2013), cap. 12, lec. 2 (hereafter, *Super Matthaeum*).

[30] Matt 12:32 (emphasis mine).

[31] Gregory the Great, *Dialogues*, trans. Odo John Zimmerman, O.S.B., ed. Roy Joseph Deferrari, Fathers of the Church 39 (New York: Fathers of the Church, Inc., 1959), lib. 4, cap. 39. "In qua senenia datur intelligi quasdam culpas in hoc saeculo, quasdam vero in futuro posse laxari. Quod enim de uno negatur, consequens intellectus patet, quia de quibusdam conceditur. Sed tamen, ut praedixi, hoc de parvis minimisque peccatis fieri posse credendum est, sicut est assiduus otiosus sermo, immoderatus risus, vel peccatum curae rei familiaris . . . cuncta etiam post mortem gravant, si adhuc in hac vita positis minime fuerint relaxata." Gregory the Great, *Dialogorum Libri IV*, Patrologia Latina 77, ed. J. P. Migne (Paris: Petit-Moutrouge, 1849).

as "temporal punishment." However, even this will need some explanation and will not be fully justified until later in this book.

In the common conception, the two components of sin are guilt (addressed above) and its consequences. This rightly corresponds to the two irreducible and exhaustive categories of evil in moral agents identified by Aquinas, fault (*culpa*) and punishment (*poena*),[32] which refer to "an evil that wounds the action or operation of beings—*evil of action*—and evil which wounds the being itself of the agent—*evil of being*."[33] Furthermore, ordinary human experience shows that some evil of being, some wound or injury in the most generic sense, always follows from evil of action. There is no such thing as a harmless evil deed. In the Christian life, we see that even after sins are forgiven some consequences remain. As I claimed above, these consequences are referred to collectively as "temporal punishment," and this concept forms the basis of every understanding of purgatory. However, as I will here begin to show, such a concept is in need of greater specification if we are to understand the true nature of human eschatological purification and which imperfections are actually being addressed in that process. Thus, we must examine and evaluate each of the various consequences of sin as potential objects of purgatorial purification.

Consequences of Original Sin

Central to Aquinas's claim that every evil in a moral agent can be reduced either to evil of fault or evil of punishment is his recognition of the implications of original sin. Such a claim would be absurd without this reference point. Common experience is enough to show that not every evil suffered by man can be directly referred to a specific fault. So much of the Bible is aimed at addressing just this problem. In the Gospel, in particular, our Lord rebuked such simplistic parallelism: "Do you think that these Galileans were worse sinners than all the other Galileans, because they suffered thus?"[34]

---

[32] Something like "just consequence" would probably be a more appropriate word, although Aquinas does frequently use "*poena*." However, as he says in *On Evil*, q. 5, a. 4, "We should note that there are two kinds of punishment: one, indeed, as a penalty for sin, the second as something concomitant" (Sed sciendum est, quod duplex est poena. Una quidem quasi taxata pro peccato, alia vero concomitans). Thomas Aquinas, *On Evil*, trans. Richard Regan, ed. Brian Davies, (New York: Oxford University Press, 2003) (hereafter, *De malo*). The category of just consequence seems to capture this dual meaning better in English.

[33] Jacques Maritain, *St. Thomas and the Problem of Evil* (Milwaukee, WI: Marquette University Press, 1942), 20. Cf. *De malo*, q. 1, a. 4.

[34] Luke 13:2.

Nevertheless, due to the justice of God, in the case of moral agents the evil of being (which here is called punishment) must always be referred to a prior fault.[35] In his supreme providence, in other words, God would not allow evil to befall human beings if it were not related to some antecedent evil action. Aquinas explains that "the tradition of faith holds that rational creatures would be unable to incur any harm, whether regarding the soul or the body or external things, except because of a previous moral fault, whether in the person or at least in human nature."[36] This concurs with the belief that, prior to the Fall, man was endowed with certain preternatural gifts that protected him from the evils that appear "natural" in the current state of man. However, after Adam's sin, the human situation changed. As God warned Adam and Eve, "for in the day that you eat of [the tree] you shall die."[37] This consequent "dying" accounts for so many of man's sufferings that do not appear attributable to specific personal faults. In fact, according to Aquinas, bodily death and "all such ills of our present life" can be referred to original sin as their cause.[38]

Additionally, it should be clarified that, in important ways, this is an extended use of the term "punishment." In the section of the *Summa* on punishment as a consequence of sin, Aquinas explains that some suffering "is not referred to sin as [its] cause, except in a restricted sense."[39] Here he specifically has in mind certain things that result from or are associated with the "corruption of nature which is itself the punishment of original sin."[40] This is the case, for instance, when one must take a bitter medicine. Taking the medicine is something evil. It is not a punishment in the strict sense, however, but only by a broad use of the term; there is no personal, human fault we can refer back to as its cause. Rather, its necessity follows as a result of the fallen condition of human nature, which is the most basic punishment of original sin. This reality, as our Lord rightly reminds us, greatly restricts our ability to identify suffering and sin on any practical level. The corruption or disordering of human nature (as will be explained more clearly below) naturally will have diverse effects in individual people according to their circumstances. Aquinas writes, "Accordingly, when original justice is removed,"

---

[35] *De malo,* q. 1, a. 4.

[36] *De malo,* q. 1, a. 4: "Habet autem hoc traditio fidei, quod nullum nocumentum creatura rationalis potuisset incurrere neque quantum ad animam, neque quantum ad corpus, neque quantum ad aliqua exteriora, nisi peccato praecedente vel in persona vel saltem in natura."

[37] Gen 2:17.

[38] *De malo,* q. 5, a. 4: "alii defectus huius vitae."

[39] *ST* Ia-Iiae, q. 87, a. 7: "non reducuntur ad culpam sicut ad causam, nisi pro tanto."

[40] *ST* Ia-Iiae, q. 87, a. 7: "est ex corruptione naturae, quae est poena originalis peccati."

as the punishment of original sin, "the nature of the human body is left to itself, so that according to diverse natural temperaments, some men's bodies are subject to more defects, some to fewer, although original sin is equal in all."[41] Thus, on one level, we need look no further than material conditions to explain why a given man is born blind, for example.[42]

Similarly, this nuance allows us to apply the broad sense of the term punishment even to those evils simply permitted by the Lord. Although Aquinas, and the broader Augustinian tradition along with him, would call them *poenae*, we need not think of the torture of innocent prisoners or the horrific examples of ethnic genocide in the last century, for example, as direct expressions of God's just punishment. Rather, this usage of *poena* only serves to show that the situation is not completely arbitrary and is only possible on the condition of a fallen state of humanity. In other words, these events fall within God's providential care of the cosmos although he nevertheless remains innocent of the particular malicious uses of man's freedom. He allows them, but only, as we know, because he is capable of bringing good from them. As St. Paul reminds us, "We know that in everything God works for good with those who love him."[43] Keeping that clarification in mind, however, we can still call them punishments in this extended use of the term.

Importantly, this clarification also provides the foundation for explaining the suffering of our Lord and our Lady, who did not sin personally and were also both conceived without original sin. Their situation is certainly unique, but our analysis has already shown that, while not denying the connection between every evil of being (punishment) and evil of action (fault), not every evil suffered must strictly be connected to a personal fault. Though not guilty themselves, they were nevertheless born into the human situation that resulted from original sin. This connects to the fault "at least in human nature" of *De malo,* question 1, article 4, cited above. A more thorough analysis of the challenges that arise from their unique situation would certainly be interesting but is beyond the scope of this book. It is only necessary to have signaled the beginnings of the explanation because otherwise their situation could present a significant objection to the essential thesis that every punishment is connected to a prior fault.

Nevertheless, having made these clarifications for the purpose of our

---

[41] *ST* Ia-Iiae, q. 85, a. 5, ad 1: "Sic igitur, remota originali iustitia, natura corporis humani relicta est sibi, et secundum hoc, secundum diversitatem naturalis complexionis, quorundam corpora pluribus defectibus subiacent, quorundam vero paucioribus, quamvis existente originali peccato aequali."

[42] Cf. John 9:1–12.

[43] Rom 8:28.

present discussion, it is clear that bodily corruption (with its accompanying ills that ultimately terminate in death) does not remain with us after this life, for it itself is the very cause of our departure. Hence, it cannot remain as something to be purified in purgatory.

Additionally, as I alluded to above, even beyond physical death the Church has always understood that on its deepest level the consequence of sin is spiritual, a kind of death to the soul that is often called the *poena damni* or the eternal loss of the beatific vision. As St. Paul's famous line teaches, "the wages of sin is death."[44] From the moment of Adam's sin all of humanity was cut off from the loving communion with God in which the first man was created. This is a worse consequence than any imaginable physical ailment. To overcome this chasm, man must receive a new infusion of gratuitous sanctifying grace. However, as I argued in the section on mortal sin, our question presumes that the soul has, in fact, received such a gift and perseveres in it. Thus, souls in purgatory do not suffer this punishment.[45]

These two punishments, namely the temporal ills of this life culminating in bodily death and the eternal death of damnation if original sin is not remitted by sanctifying grace, are the only ones mentioned by Aquinas in his treatment of the punishment of original sin in *De malo*.[46] If these are truly the only punishments, then our analysis has shown that the consequences of original sin have nothing to do with purgatory strictly speaking. However, in the *Summa* Aquinas does list another consequence, namely, the four wounds of nature: weakness, ignorance, malice, and concupiscence.[47] These, then, deserve a closer treatment.

The Wounds of Original Sin

The four wounds of nature each correspond to one of the soul's powers— malice to the will, ignorance to the intellect, weakness to the irascible appetite, and concupiscence to the concupiscible appetite. According to Aquinas, these wounds are the disorder that was inflicted on the whole of human nature as a result of the sin of our first parents.[48] In broad terms, this Fall is referred to as the loss of original justice, a systemic disordering that took place in human nature as a result of sin. It is the loss of what William

---

[44] Rom 6:23.

[45] At least eternally. The delay of the beatific vision that they experience can also be called the *poena damni,* as will be discussed in chapter four.

[46] *De malo*, q. 5.

[47] *ST* Ia-Iiae, q. 85, a. 3.

[48] *ST* Ia-Iiae, q. 85, a. 3.

A. Van Roo, S.J., describes as "the perfect rectitude of human nature, the complete subjection of the body and the lower powers of the soul to reason, and of the reason to God."[49] We have already alluded to the disorder that resulted from original sin on the predominantly material level, but here we see the corresponding spiritual consequences. In all those who inherit original sin, these powers are diminished in their proper natural ordering to virtue.[50] Reinhard Hütter describes this well:

> The wound of *ignorance* pertains to reason, in which prudence resides. Reason is weakened in its perception of the order to the true, especially in regard to moral matters—that is, the unambiguous perception of the precepts of the natural law and the proper specification of actions according to them. The wound of *malice* pertains to the will, in which justice resides: the will is weakened in its orientation to the true good. The wound of *weakness* pertains to the irascible sense appetite, in which fortitude resides and which is weakened in its orientation to overcoming what is arduous. The wound of *concupiscence* pertains to the concupiscible sense appetite, in which temperance resides. The concupiscible sense appetite is weakened in its proper orientation to the delectable moderated by reason.[51]

These wounds are certainly imperfections and belong to the evil of being referred to above. Further, since the powers are rooted in the soul[52] and are not fully perfected by baptism, as is clear to any baptized person trying to live a holy life, some of these wounds may survive the death of the body if not healed during one's lifetime.

To be clear, however, any residual wounding relevant to purgatory could only include the wounds in the purely spiritual faculties of the soul: intellect and will. Although the sensitive faculties exist *in radice* (in root) in the soul,

---

[49] William A. Van Roo, S.J., *Grace and Original Justice according to St. Thomas*, Analecta Gregoriana 75 (Rome: Apud Aedes Universitatis Gregorianae, 1955), 196. In this work Van Roo argues that, while Thomas accepts the classic "threefold subjection" characteristic of the original state of man, he ultimately believes that the subjection of reason to God was due to the gift of sanctifying grace and not original justice per se. Thus, according to Van Roo, original justice, strictly speaking, only includes the subjection of the lower powers and the body to reason. See Van Roo, *Grace and Original Justice*, 30.

[50] *ST* Ia-Iiae, q. 85, a. 3.

[51] Reinhard Hütter, "Human Sexuality in a Fallen World: An Economy of Mercy and Grace," *Nova et Vetera* 15, no. 2 (2017): 433–64, 458.

[52] *ST* Ia, q. 77.

their subject is the composite human being, body and soul. They cease to exist in act, therefore, in the separated soul. As Daniel D. De Haan and Brandon Dahm aptly explain, "The sentient powers have the rational soul and body of the hylomorphic composite as their subject, but the intellectual powers—possible intellect, agent intellect, and will—have only the rational soul and not the hylomorphic composite as their immediate subject."[53] Thus, inasmuch as the wounding of these spiritual faculties remains after death, we have identified the second genuine object of purgatorial purification.

In one sense, the next logical step would be to bring greater clarity to the nature of these wounds, but Aquinas rightly points out that they are not fundamentally different from the spiritual imperfections that arise from actual sins committed during one's life.[54] This is perhaps why Aquinas did not mention them in the *De malo* question referred to above. This disordering is not merely or exclusively the consequence of original sin but also of all of our actual sins. We are not only wounded in this way from birth, in other words, but throughout the course of our life may continue to weaken ourselves by sin. Thus, only once we have seen these wounds in that context will we be able to fully understand their nature.

Before moving on to actual sin, however, it is helpful to mention one further point about the wounds of original sin for the sake of completeness. In the Christian tradition, sometimes the term "concupiscence" is used to refer to all the wounds in a generic sense. According to Aquinas, this is because the "inordinateness of the other powers of the soul consists chiefly in their turning inordinately to [a] mutable good."[55] Hence they are called generally concupiscence. At other times this reality is also referred to as the *fomes peccati.*

These two terms tend to be used interchangeably, but it is helpful to see the difference. While in a sense speaking about the same thing, the term *fomes* refers more specifically to the "disorder of the lower parts of the soul and of the body itself."[56] In other words, *fomes* more specifically connotes the wounds of concupiscence and weakness from the perspective of their material dimension. This is because they reside in the concupiscible and irascible appetites, which have a more direct relationship to the body. In fact,

---

[53] David D. De Haan and Brandon Dahm, "Thomas Aquinas on Separated Souls as Incomplete Human Persons," *The Thomist* 83, no. 4 (2019): 589–637, 605. Cf. Thomas Aquinas, *De anima*, q. 1.

[54] *ST* Iia-Iiae, q. 85, a. 3.

[55] *ST* Ia-Iiae, q. 82, a. 3: "Inordinatio autem aliarum virium animae praecipue in hoc attenditur, quod inordinate convertuntur ad bonum commutabile."

[56] *ST* Ia-Iiae, q. 81, a. 3, ad 2: "inordinatio inferiorum partium animae et ipsius corporis."

the body-soul composite is the subject of these powers, properly speaking. This is an important distinction. Although the spiritual dimension of the wounds in these powers may be healed significantly during this life as one acquires greater and greater virtue, there is a sense in which, to the extent that these wounds dwell in the body, they will never be completely overcome in this life.[57] It is simply a fact of the current disordered state of human nature that the body and the lower powers are never fully rectified in their material dimension, even though the soul itself might acquire the proper virtues. St. Paul himself identifies this when he writes, "For I delight in the law of God, in my inmost self, but I see in my members another law at war with the law of my mind and making me captive to the law of sin which dwells in my members."[58]

As important as this point is for the spiritual life, however, it does not bear directly on the nature of purification after death. As we will see in more detail in chapter four, the separated soul in purgatory is no longer in the body and so is freed both from St. Paul's "law of sin in [his] members" and from the activity of the sense faculties. From a material perspective, therefore, he merely awaits the glorious resurrected body that will be perfectly ordered to the soul.

Consequences of Actual Sins

Having thus established the various consequences of original sin, it is now appropriate to examine their complements in the order of actual personal sins committed during one's life. While it is true that there is not a perfect identity, there is a great similarity. The first consequence mentioned above was that of physical death (with its accompanying ills). Always keeping in mind the real danger of any kind of simplistic parallelism here, at least in principle, it is possible to affirm some connection between personal sin and physical suffering in this life. Aquinas himself claims that "often bodily diseases are caused by spiritual sins."[59] We can think of many obvious examples such as the deleterious effects of alcohol and drug addictions, the proliferation of sexually transmitted diseases, or the wounds of self-mutilation. In these cases, the connection between sin and its physical consequences is undeniable.

Admittedly, however, Aquinas does seem to have even more in mind. Many biblical passages do unambiguously connect physical sufferings with

---

57 *ST* Ia-Iiae, q. 74, a. 3, ad 2.

58 Rom 7:22–23.

59 *Super Matthaeum*, cap. 8, lec. 3: "quia plerumque ex peccatis spiritualibus causantur aegritudines corporales." Cf. *Super Matthaeum*, cap. 9, lec. 1.

sins in a way that is not based on a purely natural, inherent link. In this vein we can think of numerous examples from the Old Testament such as the destruction of Sodom and Gomorrah[60] or the attack of the serpents in the desert.[61] There is also the case of Ananias and Sapphira in the Acts of the Apostles.[62] In these examples spiritual sins result in physical suffering in a way that goes beyond the merely natural consequences of the actions. Nevertheless, it must never be forgotten that it is always extremely dangerous to attempt to identify a connection in any particular case. Our Lord's warning is very clear on this point, but such practical caution is different than theoretically acknowledging the possibility. Such a connection is typically only permissible under the inspiration of God, as these biblical passages suggest, but it can, nevertheless, exist. Be that as it may, as was said in this context earlier, the corporeal consequences of sin are not directly related to purgatory and so remain outside the scope of this book.

Similarly, spiritual death is a consequence of original sin and is also certainly a consequence of actual mortal sin as well. While one can speak of this in terms of the loss of sanctifying grace and the beatific vision, it is also possible to refer to it with a common theological metaphor about the internal loss of beauty of the human soul. Aquinas calls this a "stain" or *macula*.[63] He explains this image from the premise that man's soul has a twofold "comeliness" deriving from the refulgence of the light of reason and of divine light, namely wisdom and grace, but when man sins he "cleaves to certain things, against the light of reason and of the Divine law."[64] A luminous beauty is lost and the result can thus be called a stain. Although the description seems to permit a certain amount of gradation, Aquinas explains later that *macula*, properly speaking, only refers to the loss of beauty resulting from the loss of charity.[65] It is all or nothing. Since venial sin does not destroy or even diminish charity, the effect of venial sin cannot, therefore, be called a stain in this way.[66] Nevertheless, Aquinas is willing to admit a certain similarity "insofar as [venial sin] hinders the comeliness that results from acts of virtue."[67] In other words, venial sin does not alter the habitual beauty of the soul but merely mars its actual beauty in a given moment. This distinction, however, simply

---

[60] Gen 19:12–29.

[61] Num 21:1–9.

[62] Acts 5:1–11.

[63] *ST* Ia-IIae, q. 86, a. 1.

[64] *ST* Ia-IIae, q. 86, a. 1: "adhaeret rebus aliquibus contra lumen rationis et divinae legis."

[65] *ST* Ia-IIae, q. 89, a. 1.

[66] O'Brien, "Remission of Venial Sin," 26.

[67] *ST* Ia-IIae, q. 89, a. 1: "inquantum impedit nitorem qui est ex actibus virtutum."

points us back to the need for the forgiveness of all remaining venial sins, as discussed above. Thus, our current investigation can remove *macula* from the objects of purgatorial purification, for as soon as charity returns to the soul (a prerequisite for entering purgatory) the stain is immediately removed.

Evil Dispositions

We can now return to the wounds of original sin to see them as consequences of actual sins committed in one's life. As will become clear, this is a helpful shift in arriving at a clearer account of their nature. Although we can affirm them as consequences of original sin as was done above, they are more easily understood in the context of actual sin.

In question eighty-five of the *prima secundae* of his *Summa*, Aquinas asks whether sin diminishes the good of nature.[68] As should be no surprise, a few distinctions are required to answer the question correctly. He explains that the good of nature is threefold: the good of the principles of which nature is constituted and the properties that flow from them, the natural inclination to virtue, and the gift of original justice.[69] While the gift of original justice was lost by original sin, the goodness of nature in itself can never be lost. The natural inclination to virtue, however, is not lost but "diminished by sin."[70] It is already clear from this brief description that he is speaking of the same reality as the wounds of nature discussed above.[71] In fact, Aquinas's argument cited on that point is from the same question in the *Summa*, only two articles later. Here, however, there is a more direct connection to actual sins committed.

Aquinas explains that this diminishment results from the fact that "human acts produce an inclination to like acts."[72] In other words, with each sin committed the person grows in his inclination to sinful acts. In the worst case, a habit is formed, and since it is ordered to sinful acts (or, rather, disordered) it is called "vice."[73] Furthermore, since vices are contrary to virtue and to the natural inclination of the powers of the soul, as the vices increase, the proper virtues of the soul are diminished. As the soul commits more and more sins, venial or mortal, the soul acquires greater and greater disorder in its powers. What began as a wound from original sin becomes a debilitating disease as long as a life of sin is tolerated.

---

68 *ST* Ia-Iiae, q. 85, a. 1.
69 *ST* Ia-Iiae, q. 85, a. 1.
70 *ST* Ia-Iiae, a. 85, a. 1: "diminuitur per peccatum."
71 Cf. Hütter, "Human Sexuality," 458, where he also explicitly connects the two.
72 *ST* Ia-Iiae, q. 85, a. 1: "Per actus enim humanos fit quaedam inclinatio ad similes actus."
73 *ST* Ia-Iiae, q. 54, a. 3.

Charity, however, is directly opposed to this tendency and wages a war against these disorders. Since it orders all the acts of man properly to God as his final end,[74] it is ultimately incompatible with vice. In a strict sense, when God grants the grace of charity to a soul, the vices are destroyed. A fundamental ordering to God and disordering away from him are mutually exclusive. However, as anyone can attest, some amount of conflict almost always still remains. While these inclinations no longer completely derail the soul in its pursuit of God, they constantly provoke minor deviations. This, as we have seen, is the very nature of venial sin.[75] It is for this reason that Aquinas prefers to call the perverse inclinations that remain in the soul, either after mortal sins have been forgiven or that result from venial sins, something "after the manner of dispositions" rather than "habits" (vices) in the strict sense.[76] As he explains, "They remain weakened and diminished, so as not to domineer over man."[77] He refers to these here as the "remnants of sin."[78] These remnants begin as wounds resulting from original sin at the moment of the soul's creation and grow or diminish as the soul fights against such errant tendencies. However, if they are not completely overcome in this life, then they must be healed (at least in the spiritual faculties) after death before the soul can truly be fit to enter into its eternal reward.[79]

It is helpful here to make one additional clarification that integrates what has been said until this point. When first presenting them, I spoke about the wounds in nature that result from original sin as a consequence of the loss of original justice. This is true if we speak of original justice in a broad sense as the prelapsarian perfection of human nature (though still in distinction from grace). In the passage quoted at the beginning of this section, however, the diminishment of the natural inclination to virtue (which Aquinas identifies with the wounds of nature) is distinguished from the loss of original justice.[80] The inclination to virtue was the second good

---

[74] *ST* IIa-IIae, q. 23, a. 8.

[75] *ST* Ia-IIae, q. 88, a. 1.

[76] *ST* IIIa, q. 86, a. 5: "per modum dispositionum."

[77] *ST* IIIa, q. 86, a. 5. "Remanent tamen debilitatae et diminutae, ita quod homini non dominentur."

[78] *ST* IIIa, q. 86, a. 5: "peccati reliquiae."

[79] Garrigou-Lagrange, *Life Everlasting*, 181–82.

[80] Although I am here distinguishing them, in *ST* Ia-IIae, q. 85, a. 3 (cited in footnote 54), Aquinas does directly link the wounds of original sin, here identified with the diminishment of the natural inclination to virtue, with the loss of original justice. Nevertheless, I believe *ST* Ia-IIae, q. 85, a. 1 (cited in footnote 74), which identifies the threefold good of nature, expresses Aquinas's more elaborated thought where the two goods are certainly related but nevertheless distinct. However, there is also arguably a sense in which the disordering within the powers results from

of nature. Original justice was the third. As we saw, original justice was lost while the inclination to virtue was only *diminished*.

The key distinction is that the diminishment of the natural virtuous inclination is a loss specific to a particular power, while the loss of original justice is a lack of harmony *between* reason and the lower elements of human nature. The confusion between the two losses of natural goodness (virtuous inclination in the powers and the order between reason and the lower powers) arises in the moral life, where they overlap significantly. A temptation to gluttony, for example, comes from both dimensions. Not only is there a disorder between the body, the sensitive appetite, and the governing reason, but also, in many of us, there is a kind of weakness in the concupiscible appetite itself. The disorder between them is a result of the loss of original justice. The "weakness" of the power itself, which should really be called "concupiscence" in this case, is the result of the diminishment of the natural inclination to virtue.

This distinction helps to clarify an important point. While there really can be the acquisition of genuine virtue in the powers of the soul, in our fallen condition there will not be perfect harmony between the body, the various lower powers, and the reason during this life. This is why original justice was considered a *preternatural* gift. The harmony is not an intrinsic part of the nature but must be supplied.[81] Said differently, the second good of nature enumerated above (orientation to the good of virtue) can be regained, but the third (complete harmony between all of man's powers) cannot, short of an extraordinary gratuitous gift of God.

Maintaining the difference between these two goods is essential to giving a credible account of virtue in the current human condition. Because of our fallen state, there will always be some residual internal conflict in the pursuit of the good due to the loss of original justice. Outside of a special grace from God, some amount of disharmony will always remain during this life. Nevertheless, that reality still does not negate the real possibility of perfecting the powers in virtue. Even in the midst of internal conflict, genuine virtue can be attained. That being said, if the spiritual powers of the soul are not thus perfected by virtue in this life, their residual evil dispositions will have to be overcome in purgatory.

---

the disorder between reason and the lower powers, such that principally the loss of original justice also accounts for the disorder internal to the powers.

[81] Hütter, "Human Sexuality," 456; Van Roo, *Grace and Original Justice*, 28.

Remorse

For the sake of completeness, it is necessary to mention another of the immanent consequences of sin—remorse or a sense of guilt. Unlike the weakening
of man's faculties, this consequence is self-imposed, even if somewhat involun-
tarily. When a man's conscience judges that he has performed an evil action, it
usually triggers a feeling of sorrow. It is a kind of interior self-punishment. Much
more will be said later about remorse as a means of making satisfaction for sin,
but little need be said about it here since, in itself, it is not an obstacle that
must be overcome. Far from impeding man's relationship with God, remorse
is helpful to the soul when it leads to contrition and reparation. In that sense,
proper remorse is no obstacle at all. When man's situation is finally resolved in
the joy of heaven, remorse will also naturally cease. There will be no more need
for sorrow. Thus, proper remorse is not an object for purgatorial purification.

Improper remorse or inordinate remorse, on the other hand, insofar as it
is voluntary, is a sin and even when involuntary is likely due to a residual evil
disposition causing an errant judgment. In that case, it is the underlying evil
disposition that would need to be healed and not the remorse itself. Thus,
the consequence of sin in the category of remorse only points us back to evil
dispositions as far as the objects of purification in purgatory are concerned.

Reatus Poenae

At this point it may feel like we have a complete account of those imperfections in need of purification at the end of one's life, for we have already
examined the consequences of original sin and their parallels in the case of
actual sin. In so doing, I identified the guilt of venial sins not yet forgiven
and the immanent consequences of both original sin and actual sin that
still remain in the soul as the potential objects of postmortem purification.
Aquinas, however, still lists another among the consequences of sin to be
remedied after this life: the *reatus poenae* or the debt of punishment. He
explains that it sometimes happens that "after guilt is effaced through contrition, the debt of punishment [*reatus poenae*] is not entirely taken away,"
and since "God's justice requires that sin be ordered by due punishment, a
person who dies after contrition and absolution for sin but before making
due satisfaction must be punished after this life."[82] This debt of punishment
is an obligation of the sinner before divine justice.[83]

---

[82] *Super Sent.*, lib. 4, dist. 21, q. 1, a. 1, qc. 1: "Si enim per contritionem deleta culpa non tollitur
ex toto reatus poenae . . . justitia Dei hoc exigit ut peccatum per poenam debitam ordinetur;
oportet quod ille qui post contritionem de peccato et absolutionem decedit ante satisfactionem
debitam, quod post hanc vitam puniatur."

[83] Garrigou-Lagrange, *Life Everlasting*, 158–59.

The objection immediately arises that perhaps this debt of punishment is merely the same thing as the inherent consequences of sin, only considered from a divine rather than a human perspective. This objection will be considered in much more detail in the following chapters, but it is essential at least to acknowledge it now to be sure we have correctly identified the outline of the topic. Certainly, as I alluded to above, all the consequences of sin are a kind of punishment, but it is nevertheless essential to maintain their fundamental irreducibility. In Aquinas's mind, the immanent consequences of sin and the punishment to be endured are not identical.

The key is that, while the evil dispositions are a direct result of sin, in the case of the *reatus poenae* there is a distinction between the debt of punishment and the punishment itself. By the very fact that he commits a sin, according to Aquinas, man becomes deserving of punishment. In this sense, the *reatus poenae*, like the evil dispositions, is a direct consequence of sin. The punishment to be endured, however, is a distinct effect. As Aquinas explains, punishment is an effect of sin, "*not directly* but dispositively."[84] Sin, in other words, "makes man *deserving of punishment*" but does not cause this punishment as one of its direct consequences.[85] God or one of his instruments must intervene in order to bring it about.

It follows that the punishment due to sin cannot be strictly identified with the evil dispositions presented above, since these latter are among the direct, immanent consequences of sin. Aquinas's logic excludes this possibility. To put it simply, the basic claim of Aquinas is that there is a logical, if not often real, distinction between the particular immanent consequences of sin and the punishment before God that the sinner must endure. This is a controversial claim, especially in the contemporary context, and one that deserves thorough analysis. The implications for purgatory, however, are straightforward. If the requisite punishment before divine justice is not sufficiently borne during one's earthly life, it must be completed in purgatory. If we accept Aquinas's distinction, then, we have identified three objects of purgatorial purification: the guilt of venial sins not yet forgiven, evil dispositions still remaining in the soul, and a debt of punishment to be satisfied or expiated before divine justice.

---

[84] *ST* I-IIae, q. 87, a. 1, ad 2: "non est effectus peccati directe, sed solum dispositive" (emphasis added).

[85] *ST* I-IIae, q. 87, a. 1, ad 2: "facit hominem esse reum poenae" (emphasis added).

CONCLUSION

It is important to recognize that this distinction between the immanent consequences of sin and the punishment to be endured was widely received in the tradition of the Church by many who would not consider themselves exclusive followers of Aquinas. St. Robert Bellarmine, for example, in his work on purgatory identifies four remnants of sin.[86] However, *fomes* is on his list, and he admits that it is "certainly abolished in death."[87] The remaining three are "bad habits," "venial sins," and "the undergoing of temporal punishments."[88] The harmony with Aquinas is obvious. Even many centuries later, a leading purgatory scholar of the early twentieth century, Martin Jugie, taught that "[a] soul may go to purgatory, then for three reasons: 1° on account of venial sins not remitted here on earth; 2° on account of vicious inclinations left in the soul through the habits of sin; 3° on account of the temporal punishment due to every sin, mortal or venial, committed after Baptism and not sufficiently atoned for during life."[89] Here again is a confirmation of what came to be the predominant theological consensus. Nevertheless, this account has not been without its objectors, even from the earliest days. In particular, there has always been criticism of the idea of a *reatus poenae*, especially from Orthodox and Protestant perspectives. Thus, in the next chapter I will examine these objections and highlight the relevant issues at stake for our Thomistic account of purgatory.

---

[86] Robert Bellarmine, S.J., *De Controversiis: On Purgatory*, trans. Ryan Grant (Post Falls, ID: Mediatrix Press, 2017), 197–99.

[87] Bellarmine, *On Purgatory*, 198.

[88] Bellarmine, *On Purgatory*, 197.

[89] Martin Jugie, *Purgatory and the Means to Avoid It* (Cork, Ireland: Mercier Press, 1949), 4.

CHAPTER II

Objections to the Three Objects of Purgatorial Purification

IN THE PRECEDING CHAPTER, I identified three distinct objects of purification in purgatory. Although there has been a general consensus among Catholic theologians, none of the objects, unsurprisingly, have been without their critics. The debates between Catholics, Orthodox, and Protestants on the issue have been the most noteworthy in the history of the doctrine, but there have also been some divergences among Catholic theologians. I will present the objections here as they correspond to the three objects identified. I do not intend to address the Thomistic response to them in this chapter, however, but merely to identify the particular points of contention. Highlighting the shape of the debates will, nevertheless, give us greater insight into the central notions of a Catholic theology of purgatory. In particular, we will see that the notion of punishment and the *reatus poenae* is at the heart of the doctrine. This is the principal object of purification for the Catholic theologians and the primary point of disagreement for the Orthodox and Protestants. A survey of these positions will thus clarify the questions that the Thomistic account will need to address in the systematic recapitulation of the following two chapters.

UNFORGIVEN VENIAL SINS

An interesting objection to the first object is found in a theory proposed by the famous thirteenth-century Franciscan theologian Bl. John Duns Scotus. He does not argue that venial sins do not still need to be forgiven after death. Rather, he suggests that the forgiveness of venial sins simply is the satisfaction of the *reatus poenae*. In his *Ordinatio* he writes, "it can be said in one way that the remission of venial [sin] is nothing other than the payment [*solutio*] of the temporal punishment due to it. This is proven since, after the transitory act, the guilt which remains is nothing but the debt of punishment owed: the guilt of venial sin is nothing but the debt of temporal punishment."[1] Scotus argues, in other words, that the first and third objects (*reatus culpae* and *reatus poenae*, respectively) are really the same thing and that the first can be collapsed into the third. An unforgiven sin is just a sin that has not been punished yet. As O'Brien explains, "the approach of Scotus seems to lack a distinction between the condition of guilt and liability to punishment."[2] Guilt for a venial sin is the temporal punishment still owed. When the punishment has been satisfied, the sin is forgiven ipso facto. Thus, Scotus is content to argue that, in fact, many venial sins are forgiven in purgatory. He writes, "And consequently, once the temporal punishment for this sin is satisfied [*soluta*] in purgatory, by this very thing the guilt itself of the venial sin is remitted."[3] Conversely, according to this line of reasoning, what he would not say is that someone might still have to suffer punishment for a sin already forgiven.

Certain unique conclusions follow from the position suggested by Scotus. Because it does not acknowledge a difference between guilt and the debt of punishment, a venial sin can be forgiven without any specific movement back toward God.[4] In fact, it follows that, irrespective of the presence or absence of sanctifying grace, many venial sins can be forgiven merely through unfortunate life circumstances without the sinner ever making a single act of love for God or repentance for those sins. If forgiveness is simply the suffering of an adequate punishment, then grace is not required. This is remarkably different from Aquinas, who argued, as we saw, that forgiveness

---

[1] John Duns Scotus, *Ordinatio Liber Quartus: A Distinctione Decima Quarta ad Quadragesimam Secundam,* in *Opera Omnia,* vol. 13 (Vatican City: Typis Vaticanis, 2011), d. 21, q. 1: "Potest dici uno modo sic, quod nihil aliud est culpae venialis remissio quam solutio poenae temporalis debitae pro ea. Probatur, quia post actum transeuntem culpa—quae manet—nihil est nisi reatus ad poenam debitam; ille autem reatus venialis non est nisi reatus ad poenam temporalem" (all translations of Scotus are mine). Admittedly, Scotus is highly nuanced on this matter, and it is not clear that he was genuinely committed to this theory. There is reason to believe this is just an option he was considering. In any case, identifying Scotus's definitive position would require a much more thorough investigation and is not my intention. For our purposes it is enough to contrast a possibility suggested by Scotus with the position held by Aquinas.

[2] O'Brien, "Remission of Venial Sin," 33.

[3] Scotus, d. 21, q. 1: "Et per consequens, soluta poena temporali in purgatorio pro isto veniali, ex hoc ipso ista culpa venialis remissa est."

[4] O'Brien, "Remission of Venial Sin," 33.

of venial sin comes through an act of fervent love for God, which could not be possible without the presence of habitual charity.[5]

Admittedly, Scotus would agree that such an act of fervor could forgive sin. He writes, "venial sins are destroyed at any time both with respect to guilt and to punishment . . . such as through a fervent act of contemplating God, just as a drop is immediately consumed by a vehement flame."[6] However, although Scotus and Aquinas are in material agreement on this particular point, there is still a deeper underlying disagreement. The important point for Aquinas is that the fervent act of charity virtually includes an act of penance, a return to God contrary to the way in which one departed from him in venial sin.[7] For Scotus, the point he is explicitly arguing here is that such an act of penance is not necessary. Just a few sentences before the section quoted above, he writes, "And no one is required [to make] any contrition for venial sins."[8] Thus, Scotus is willing to acknowledge various means of satisfying the debt of punishment. Minimally, it can be satisfied by simply bearing the punishment, or, more sweetly, it may be satisfied by acts of virtue or charity. In neither case, though, is a specific movement of penance necessary, because the guilt is simply reduced to the debt of punishment owed to divine justice. In contrast, Aquinas's insistence on at least some virtual movement of repentance as distinct from satisfaction shows the fundamental irreducibility of guilt and the debt of punishment in his mind.

The concept explained here leads Scotus to the idea that venial sin could even be forgiven in hell. He writes, "It is not unfitting for the punishment due to a venial sin to come to an end in hell."[9] If punishment is being suffered in hell, there is no reason why the requisite finite amount could not be reached and the venial sin thereby be forgiven. Nevertheless, he would not say that mortal sins could be forgiven there. He continues, "Yet, there will not be

---

[5] O'Brien, "Remission of Venial Sin," 34.

[6] Scotus, d. 17, q. 1: "venialia delentur quandoque quantum ad culpam et poenam . . . sicut per aliquem actum ferventem contemplationis in Deum, quemadmodum gutta consumitur statim a flamma vehementi." In a similar way, in d. 21, q. 1, which we have also been examining, an alternative position considered by Scotus (after he acknowledges that there are many who do distinguish between guilt and the debt punishment) is that venial sin can be remitted not by punishment but by some act more pleasing to God than our sin was displeasing. He writes, "potest dici alio modo quod peccatum veniale in vita ista remitti potest non tantum per poenam interiorem vel exteriorem, quia illa non est necessaria ad hoc, sed per aliquem actum Deo magis acceptum quam peccatum veniale displiceat."

[7] O'Brien, "Remission of Venial Sin," 39.

[8] Scotus, d. 17, q. 1: "Nec aliquis tenetur ad aliquam contritionem pro venialibus."

[9] Scotus, d. 21, q. 1: "Nec est inconveniens poenam debitam veniali habere terminum in inferno."

forgiveness in hell of that sin for which one was damned."[10] Although venial sins are forgiven in hell for Scotus, mortal sins are not. The punishment of mortal sin is such that of its very nature "it cannot be totally satisfied."[11] It is eternal and, therefore, unsatisfiable, since it is an infinite offence.

Nevertheless, according to the position of Scotus presented here, God, in his mercy, can commute the eternal punishment into a temporal one for those who are repentant in this life, "and this commutation is called the 'forgiveness' of mortal sin."[12] In other words, the "forgiveness" of mortal sin is simply God changing the punishment due for said sin into the kind that man could actually make satisfaction for. It is a sovereign act of God's will. This shows by consequence that, according to this theory, even in the case of mortal sin there is no real difference between guilt and the debt of punishment.

This, then, must be the critical point of engagement with the position suggested by Scotus. Our question becomes, what is the proportionate relationship between guilt and punishment? Can the two really be united as in the thought of Scotus, or must they remain distinguished as Aquinas teaches? A clear way to investigate this would be to analyze whether punishment ever remains after the complete forgiveness of sin. If guilt and the debt of punishment are identical, then a lack of guilt ought to mean the absence of any due punishment. However, if punishment remains after forgiveness, then the two cannot be so identified. In the next chapter I will show that in many places both Scripture and the magisterium suggest that the two categories must remain distinct. Furthermore, the systematic explanation of Aquinas which follows will then show in thorough detail exactly why this must be the case.

Evil Dispositions

Even if not all theologians consider evil dispositions explicitly, there are not any who believe in purgatory and yet deny that these imperfections are in need of purification in some way. That being said, the transformative dimension of purification was significantly minimized in the great early modern treatises on purgatory,[13] and this stance continued to influence

---

[10] Scotus, d. 21, q. 1: "Nec tamen in inferno erit redemptio illius, scilicet peccati, pro quo iste est damnatus."

[11] Scotus, d. 21, q. 1: "non potest totaliter esse soluta."

[12] Scotus, d. 21, q. 1: "et ista commutatio vocatur 'remissio' culpae mortalis."

[13] As a historical conjecture, I believe this is due to the significant debates about the role of satisfaction between Catholics and the Orthodox and Protestants (as we will see in the next

Catholic theology until relatively recent times. According to the French *Dictionnaire de Théologie Catholique*, the two most important theologians in the post-Tridentine exposition of purgatory were St. Robert Bellarmine, S.J., and Francisco Suarez, S.J.[14] They played an exceedingly important role in defending the traditional teaching on purgatory in the face of Protestant objections, and each has a sizeable treatise on the topic.

As was mentioned earlier, Bellarmine identified the same three objects of purification that we saw above. We should note, however, the way he explains the purification of the dispositions:

> Now in regard to bad habits, those which exist in the will are not necessarily extinguished by death, seeing that they are in the powers that are not bound to an organ . . . Therefore, it is believable that all these habits are abolished by the first contrary act of the separated soul, which it elicits immediately from separation. For, even if this habit, contracted in one act, cannot be destroyed by many acts, nevertheless, there it will be able to be [destroyed by that first contrary act] because the act will be much more forceful, seeing that then the soul will be more powerful in regard to spiritual acts and it will not have the contrary *fomites* and resistance as it has here. Thus, it remains to speak of suffering punishment and venial sin, which can properly be called the remainder of sin, which is the reason why Purgatory exists.[15]

Although he acknowledges the need to purify bad habits, this is taken care of immediately, and the rest of the time in purgatory is spent suffering an adequate punishment. If we were to distinguish the second and third objects (residual evil dispositions and the *reatus poenae*, respectively) along the lines of healing and retribution, Bellarmine would say that any healing that needs to happen takes place immediately, and the rest of the purgation is merely an expression of just retribution. Suarez argues similarly:

> But someone says: for obtaining beatitude it is not enough to lack all guilt and debt of punishment, but also bad habits and inclinations. I respond, it is not right to form some detention for this reason; for

---

section). Because of these controversies it became essential to defend purgatory principally on these terms.

[14] A. Michel, "Purgatoire," in *Dictionnaire de Théologie Catholique* (Paris: Libraire Letouzey et Ané, 1936), 1282.

[15] Bellarmine, *On Purgatory*, 198–99.

whatever of this is in the sense appetite, is shed with death itself, along with the body, which the appetite is in; but a habit existing in the will, is either taken away in the instant of death, or by contrary deeds performed by divine strength, or by the removal of the influx of divine conservation [of those habits], or certainly all the natural virtues are infused *per accidens* by reason of the status of the soul on its first entry into glory, and these expel the repugnant habits, just in the same way as the general sciences also, which expel every ignorance.[16]

Without offering a definitive solution, Suarez does not seem to think of the purification of these habits as forming a constitutive component of purgatory.

As I suggested above, the thought of Bellarmine and Suarez had a strong impact on Catholic theology. Jugie, for instance, taught that "neither venial sin nor vicious inclination survives the first instant that follows death."[17] In our current context, such a portrait of purgatory, although consistent with everything argued up to this point in the book, seems to strike against common Catholic sensibility. Most who have at least a vague cultural awareness of Dante's great trilogy, for example, imagine purgatory as a gradual healing process. To this concern, Dom S. Louismet in his 1919 treatise on the spiritual life wrote the following:

There are two views concerning the state of a separated soul, which has to undergo the punishment of Purgatory. The first view is that which finds favour with the popular mind; the second, that which is the expression of strict theological truth . . . The popular mind about Purgatory is that one ends there by gradually acquiring purity and saintliness, whilst the theological truth is that a man, not a reprobate at the hour of death, becomes a perfect saint the moment

---

[16] Francisco Suarez, "De Purgatorio," in *Opera Omnia*, vol. 22 (Paris: Apud Ludovicum Vives, 1861), disp. 47, §1, no. 5: "Dicet vero aliquis: ad beatitudinem obtinendam non satis est carere omni culpa et reatu poenae, sed etiam pravis habitibus et inclinationibus. Respondeo, propter hanc causam non oportere fingere detentionem aliquam; nam quidquid huiusmodi est in appetitu sentiente, in ipsa morte deponitur, simul cum corpore, in quo est appetitus; habitus vero existentes in voluntate, vel in ipso insanti mortis auferuntur, aut per actus contrarios divina virtute factos, aut per abstractionem divini influxus conservantis, aut certe in primo ingressu gloriae ratione status infunduntur per accidens omnes virtutes etiam naturales, quae habitus repugnantes expellunt, sicut infuditur etiam scientiae generales, quae omnem expellunt ignor-atiam" (translation mine).

[17] Jugie, *Purgatory*, 5.

after, whatever be his debts to the divine justice, which indeed will have to be paid to the last farthing.[18]

Louismet clearly follows the doctrine of Bellarmine, and the contrast he presents between this teaching and the opposing view is stark.

Nevertheless, although the majority did seem to accept this account, not all theologians agreed. In response, for example, M. F. Egan wrote an article in which he attempted "to support the popular view so summarily dismissed by Dom Louismet" and to show that it is in accord with Catholic teaching.[19] He aptly titled his paper "The Two Theories of Purgatory." The question for us is, which theory does Aquinas accept?

Admittedly, the answer is a debatable one. Thomists have argued on both sides of the issue. Earlier in the same section quoted above, Jugie writes, "the majority of theologians hold *with St. Thomas* that these inclinations do not survive the first instant that follows separation of soul and body."[20] Thus, it would seem that Aquinas, too, supports what was described as the "strict theological view." Unfortunately, though, Jugie does not give us a reference to verify the claim. In contrast, Garrigou-Lagrange argues the opposite. He writes:

> Do these dispositions remain in the separated soul? Yes. They are like rust, penetrating at times to the depths of the intelligence and the will. Does this rust disappear suddenly upon entrance into purgatory? Some theologians think so, because an intense act of charity can immediately take away these evil dispositions. Now *we do not find this answer in St. Thomas*, but rather its contrary.[21]

He then proceeds to quote Aquinas from the *Scriptum*, where the angelic doctor explains that "the harshness of the penalty properly corresponds to the quantity of fault, but the duration corresponds to how rooted the fault was in the subject."[22] Garrigou-Lagrange then concludes, "Now uprooting

---

18 Savinien Louismet, *Mysticism—True and False*, 2nd ed. (London: Burns & Oates Ltd.: 1919), 41–42.

19 M. F. Egan, "The Two Theories of Purgatory," *Irish Theological Quarterly* 17, no. 1 (1951): 24–34, 24.

20 Jugie, *Purgatory*, 4 (emphasis mine).

21 Garrigou-Lagrange, *Life Everlasting*, 182 (emphasis mine).

22 *Super sent.*, lib. 4, dist. 21, q. 1, a. 3, qc. 3, ad 1: "acerbitas poenae proprie respondet quantitati culpae; sed diuturnitas respondet radicationi culpae in subject."

is generally a long process, demanding a long affliction or a long penance."[23] Thus, according to Garrigou-Lagrange, Aquinas actually did support a version of the "popular view" that Louismet and Egan discussed in which the soul progressively acquires habitual moral perfection in purgatory, a view that remains significantly distinct from the tradition passed down by Bellarmine and others like him.[24]

What, then, is at stake in these two theories? As far as we have seen, there is no disagreement about the objects of purgatory but only about the timing of their purification and their proportionate relationship to one another. In an important way, then, we can say there is a fundamental agreement. As will be clear in the next chapter, both accounts accord with the essential dogmatic teaching proclaimed by the Church. Nevertheless, important differences do follow from these two positions. Most importantly, if the evil dispositions are healed in the first instant, it follows that the remaining punishment is purely retributive, not medicinal. Certainly purgatory, in the broad sense, would retain a medicinal character, but the punishments endured there would not. The person would be healed, but in a way that remained fundamentally disconnected from the punishments undergone in purgatory. Conversely, the system of Aquinas as read by Garrigou-Lagrange, while not reducing the three objects into one another, preserves the possibility of a genuinely medicinal punishment. Our systematic analysis will then have to evaluate this implication and the compatibility of either theory with a reasonable account of the faith. On this point, we will see that the recent magisterium seems to support the Thomistic position presented by Garrigou-Lagrange.

REATUS POENAE

Certainly the idea of a *reatus poenae* is the most challenging of the three objects. It does not sit comfortably with most modern readers and is in need of significant justification. It is not evident in the same way for us as it was for Aquinas why a sin already forgiven is deserving of punishment. We are all children, in a way, of Nietzsche, who argued that punishment typically results from the arbitrary imposition of the will to power by another and is ultimately morally unjustifiable, merely the expression of a desire for cruelty

---

[23] Garrigou-Lagrange, *Life Everlasting*, 182.

[24] While I agree with Garrigou-Lagrange's solution to the problem, I do not think his citation of Aquinas on this issue is conclusive. As I will argue in chapter four, I believe that that passage does allow for an alternative interpretation, one in line with the position presented by Bellarmine or Suarez. It will require more than a single citation to judge between these two theories. Such is the project of chapter four.

or control.[25] How does one evil (sin), we might ask, justify the infliction of a second (punishment)?[26] Even more moderately, we might simply ask what purpose punishment serves once the person has returned to good will as our question here presumes. The souls in purgatory are in friendship with God. Their fundamental disposition is good, and so any punishment seems merely vindictive and therefore irrational. It is no longer needed for their rehabilitation or therapeutic conversion. According to these concerns, we could never attribute punishment to God as Aquinas's account does. It seems unfitting of a truly just and good God. At most we could allow that God simply permits the undesirable consequences of sin, and we could call that "punishment" by a kind of analogy. As the following sections will show, there are many who have argued in just this way.

Orthodox

The position mentioned is far from new. Although it has gained traction in the West only in more recent times, the Orthodox have been arguing with Latin Catholics over this issue for centuries. Traditionally, the Orthodox subscribe to a non-punitive theory of purgation after this life that is not based on the demands of divine justice but on the need for personal healing and interior conversion. In other words, they deny that the *reatus poenae* as discussed in this book is an accurate or meaningful category. The debate reached an apex during the discussions at the Council of Florence. Although the majority of the Orthodox present did, in the end, formally agree with the Latin position, one significant voice refused—namely, Mark of Ephesus, also known as Mark Eugenicus, the bishop of Ephesus and a leading theological representative of the East. At the Council he was the principal Orthodox debater on this issue.

He and several Latin theologians exchanged letters and addresses in the preliminary discussions of the Council. While they could agree on certain things, such as the existence of a group of souls in a middle state (Mark calls these *hoi mesoi* [the middle ones]), the differences that emerged were significant. In particular, Mark strongly rejected the Latin idea of just satisfaction and the claim that this happens through a punishment imposed by God. In his understanding, souls in the middle state are suffering, but this is only

---

[25] Peter Koritansky, *Thomas Aquinas and the Philosophy of Punishment* (Washington, DC: The Catholic University of America Press, 2011), 2–3.

[26] I credit Serge-Thomas Bonino, O.P., for the pithy formulation of this question.

the result of their confrontation with the truth about their sinfulness and the interior sense of guilt for their sins:

> We will say therefore that the punishments, by which the middle ones are afflicted, are sorrow, or the shame or sting of conscience, or repentance, or an enclosure and darkness, or fear and ambiguity about the future, or only the delay of divine vision, by reason of faults committed by each person, and most rightly the mode of understanding and speaking will be had here.[27]

As Demetrios Bathrellos explains, "[Mark] understands the aforementioned torments as self-inflicted side-effects of the committed sins rather than as punishments imposed by divine justice for the sake of satisfaction."[28] They are simply the result of an awareness of one's moral condition. Eventually, this suffering is ended by the moral purification of the soul.

Nevertheless, there is a certain ambiguity in Mark's thought. The dynamic he identifies is connected to the remission of sin, which takes place as a kind of crowning completion, but he does not consistently explain how he understands this process. Bathrellos notes that sometimes Mark considers "the idea of purification as a prerequisite for the remission of sins."[29] One must become fully rectified in order to be forgiven. It may not be obvious at first, but the passage we saw from Mark above has this idea in the background. This is due to his firm conviction that "forgiveness and punishment cannot go together."[30] Thus, even when the punishment is exclusively self-imposed, if souls are suffering, it is because they have not yet been forgiven. According

---

[27] Mark Eugenicus, "Marci Archiepiscopi Ephesii Oratio Altera de Igne Purgatorio," in *Documents Relatifs au Concile de Florence*, Patrologia Orientalis 15, ed. And trans. Louis Petit (Turnhout: Editions Brepols, 1990), 118 (English translation mine from the Latin provided by Petit): "Λύπην ἄρα καὶ τὴν τοὺς μέσους κολάζουσαν εἶναι φήσαντες, ἢ συνειδότος αἰσχύνην καὶ βάσανον, ἢ μετάμελον, ἢ συγκλεισμὸν καὶ σκότος, ἢ φόβον καὶ ἀδηλίαν τοῦ μέλλοντος, ἢ καὶ μόνην ἀναβολὴν τῆς θείας θεωρίας, κατ' ἀναλογίαν τῶν πεπλημμελημένων αὐτοῖς, εὐλογώτατ' ἂν εἴημεν οὕτω καὶ φρονοῦντες καὶ λέγοντες"; "Dixerimus ergo poenam, qua medii afficiuntur, moerorem ese, vel conscientiae pudorem ac stimulum, vel paenitudinem, vel inclusionem et caliginem, vel pavorem ac futuri ambiguitatem, vel solam divinae visionis dilationem, pro ratione culparum ab unoquoque admissarum, et rectissimus habebitur hic sentiendi dicendique modus."

[28] Demetrios Bathrellos, "Love, Purification, and Forgiveness versus Justice, Punishment, and Satisfaction: The Debates on Purgatory and the Forgiveness of Sins at the Council of Ferrara-Florence," *The Journal of Theological Studies* 65, no. 1 (April 2014): 78–121, 90.

[29] Bathrellos, "Debates on Purgatory," 95.

[30] Mark Eugenicus, "Oratio Altera de Igne Purgatorio," 56 (English translation mine): "ἄφεσιν γὰρ καὶ κόλασιν ἐς ταὐτὸ συνελθεῖν οὐχ οἷόν τε"; "remissio et poena simul convenire non possunt."

to Bathrellos's reading, their torment "contributes to the purification of their souls, which will be *hopefully followed* by divine forgiveness."[31] The soul is suffering interiorly, then, either because it knows that it has committed "small sins" and yet has not fully repented or that it has repented from "major ones" but "without producing worthy fruits of repentance."[32] In other words, God cannot or will not forgive the morally imperfect. When Mark is read this way, forgiveness is seen as a kind of reward only obtainable by a complete conversion of heart. Forgiveness would then be consequent upon purification rather than efficacious or at least auxiliary in producing it.

More often, however, Mark seems to see forgiveness as a kind of "amnesty, which God as heavenly king grants lovingly and freely to souls in the middle state."[33] Here forgiveness is a completely gratuitous gift of God, independent of any intrinsic change in the soul. When Mark is read this way, the person can do little to obtain the desired forgiveness. The soul suffers because it has not yet been forgiven, but its suffering (which in some sections, as we saw, he calls punishment) does not lead to forgiveness per se. He argues, "for if remission is had, whether it be through prayers or solely through divine clemency, then there is no more need of supplication or purgation. If however punishment and purgation are established [by God] . . . then in vain, so it seems, we pour out prayers and praise divine mercy."[34] Forgiveness, in other words, is not obtained by suffering but only by the divine mercy requested in prayer. Suffering may lead one to prayer, but it is exclusively the prayer and not the suffering that obtains forgiveness. Mark does acknowledge that the forgiveness of sins after death "is laborious (indeed, it has a conjunction with penance and a contrite conscience and a bewailing of lost goods). Nevertheless, punishment has no direct part in it, if it is remission; for the remission [of sins] and punishment cannot go together."[35] Rather, as soon as forgiveness is obtained the "punishment"

---

[31] Bathrellos, "Debates on Purgatory," 91 (emphasis mine).

[32] Bathrellos, "Debates on Purgatory," 89.

[33] Bathrellos, "Debates on Purgatory," 95.

[34] Eugenicus, "Oratio Prima," in *Documents Relatifs au Concile de Florence*, Patrologia Orientalis 15, ed. And trans. Louis Petit (Turnhout: Editions Brepols, 1990), 45: "Εἰ μὲν γὰρ ἄφεσις ἢ δι᾽ εὐχῶν ἢ παρ᾽ κὐτῆς καὶ μόνης τῆς θείας φιλανθρωπίας, οὐκ ἔτι χρεία κολάσεως καὶ καθάρσεως· εἰ δὲ κόλασίς τε καὶ κάθαρσις ὡρισμέναι μάτην ὡς ἔοικεν αἱ εὐχαὶ γίνονται καὶ τὴν θείαν φιλανθρωπίαν ὑμνοῦμεν"; "Etenim si habeatur remissio, sive per preces ea fiat, sive per ipsam solam divinam clementiam, iam non amplius supplicio ac purgatione est opus; sin vero punitio simul ac purgatio statuantur . . . iam in vanum, ut videtur, preces fundimus divinamque laudamus misericordiam."

[35] Eugenicus, "Oratio Prima," 56: "ἐπίπονος μὲν καὶ αὐτή (τὴν γὰρ μετάνοιαν ἔχει συνεζευγμένην καὶ τὴν συνείδησιν πλήττουσαν καὶ τὴν ἀποτυχίαν τῶν ἀγαθῶν ὀδυνῶσαν), κολάσεως δὲ ἀμιγής ὅμως, εἴπερ ἐστὶν ἄφεσις· ἄφεσιν γὰρ καὶ κόλασιν ἐς ταὐτὸ συνελθεῖν οὐχ οἷόν τε"; "Laboriosa quidem et

likewise ceases. Along these lines he explains that "the remission of sins is connected to the release from the punishments due to it. At the same time that anyone is absolved from sins, he is also freed from punishments by the same act of remission."[36] In this case, purgation then comes about "not however through fire," as if by a punishment imposed by divine justice, "but only through divine mercy and goodness."[37]

In whichever way Mark is read, his fundamental convictions come to light. He does believe that some imperfect souls are suffering after death because of what we would call unforgiven venial sins or because of mortal sins that one, in some way, has not quite freed oneself from. Forgiveness, consequently, is the ultimate goal, and in some way (either as a prerequisite or as a direct consequence), it always and everywhere includes moral purification and the end of all suffering. There is no room in his mind for the idea that the punishment of the *mesoi* is imposed directly by God, that it obtains forgiveness (as the position considered by Scotus would suggest), or (even worse) that it might continue after forgiveness. At best, it may lead to a moral purification involving acts of repentance and conversion which then enable one to be forgiven. More often, however, it is merely the occasion of prayers for release. Consequently, it seems that Mark would agree to our second object of purification, remaining evil dispositions, against which one will have to struggle and which consequently contribute to the pain of these middle souls, but he would certainly not agree to our third, the *reatus poenae*. In this way, the suffering that Latins identify as the satisfaction of the debt of punishment would be subsumed as an intrinsic part of the purification of moral imperfections. Our third object (*reatus poenae*), in other words, would be reduced to the second (residual evil dispositions). What he at times permits us to call "punishment" is just the complex web of the interior and psychological consequences of sin.

This view continues to be the predominant one today in many Orthodox Churches. It would certainly be beyond the scope of this book to survey

---

ipsa est (paenitentiam enim secum habet coniunctam et conscientiam percutientem amissaque bona lugentem); est tamen poenae prorsus expers, si quidem remissio est; namque remissio et poena simul convenire non possunt."

[36] Eugenicus, "Oratio Prima," 55: "Ἔστι μὲν ἡ τῶν ἁμαρτιῶν ἄφεσις ὁμολογουμένως καὶ τῆς ἐπ᾽ αὐταῖς κολάσεως ἀπαλλαγή· ἅμα γάρ τις ἀφίεται τούτων, καὶ τῆς ὀφειλομένης δι᾽ αὐτὰς κολάσεως ἠλευθέρωται"; "Est quidem citra controversiam, peccatorum remissioni coniunctam esse liberationem a poena pro ipsis debita; simul enim ac quispiam ab eis absolvitur, a poena etiam ob eadem solvenda liberatur."

[37] Eugenicus, "Oratio Prima," 52: "οὐ μὴν τὸν διὰ πυρός, ἀλλὰ τὸν διὰ τῆς θείας εὐσπλαγχνίας καὶ ἀγαθότητος μόνον"; "non tamen per ignem, sed per divinam tantum misericordiam ac bonitatem."

accurately the full spectrum of Orthodox positions on purification after death, but the 1981 article of Metropolitan Kallistos Ware is a helpful contemporary expression.[38] Ware identifies the "notion that through [their] sufferings souls in purgatory *make satisfaction* for their sins, and that these sufferings possess an *atoning* or *expiatory* value" as one of the main contentions that the Orthodox have against the Latin teaching on purgatory.[39] He rightly recognizes that a primary source of this understanding is the distinction between the *reatus culpae* and *reatus poenae*, between guilt and the debt of punishment.[40] He explains:

> To [the] Orthodox this appears a misleading way of looking at the matter. If our offences are freely forgiven, why must we still undergo punishment for them? Someone who dies in a state of genuine repentance, but who is in other respects ill-prepared to come face to face with God, may well require to undergo purification after his death, and this purification may cause him suffering; but it makes no sense to say that he is undergoing punishment for the sins that God in his mercy has already forgiven.[41]

According to this explanation, Ware's position is somewhat closer to that of Aquinas. He is very explicit about the need to painfully overcome one's moral imperfections, our second object. There is not the same fundamental incompatibility between having obtained forgiveness and still being in a state of suffering as we saw above. Forgiveness is not delayed until the end. Nevertheless, the central issue identified by Mark of Ephesus six hundred years prior still remains pertinent today. Like Mark, Ware is vehemently opposed to the idea that satisfactory punishment from God *follows* forgiveness, and as these theologians have rightly understood, this idea is essential to the Latin teaching on purgatory. Though not exhausted by it, the Catholic conception of purgatory depends on this notion of the debt of punishment.

Protestants

The view of purification after death expressed by Ware is remarkably similar to a view that has become increasingly common in some contemporary

---

[38] Kallistos Ware, "'One Body in Christ': Death and the Communion of Saints," *Sobornost (Incorporating Eastern Churches Review)* 3, no. 2 (1981): 179–91.

[39] Ware, "Death and the Communion of Saints," 184.

[40] Ware, "Death and the Communion of Saints," 185.

[41] Ware, "Death and the Communion of Saints," 185.

Protestant circles. Traditionally, purgatory has been one of the primary points of disagreement between Catholics and Protestants. One need look no further than the famous words of John Calvin on the subject in his *Institutes of Christian Religion*:

> [W]hen the expiation of sins is sought elsewhere than in the blood of Christ, when satisfaction is transferred elsewhere . . . We must cry out with the shouting not only of our voices but of our throats and lungs that purgatory is a deadly fiction of Satan, which nullifies the cross of Christ, inflicts unbearable contempt upon God's mercy, and overturns and destroys our faith. For what means this purgatory of theirs but that satisfaction for sins is paid by the souls of the dead after their death? Hence when the notion of satisfaction is destroyed, purgatory itself is straightway torn up by the very roots. But if it is perfectly clear from our preceding discourse that the blood of Christ is the sole satisfaction for the sins of believers, the sole expiation, the sole purgation, what remains but to say that purgatory is simply a dreadful blasphemy against Christ?[42]

With his references to satisfaction it is clear that he, like the Orthodox, has the very notion of the *reatus poenae* in mind as a primary concern. Purgatory, for him, hinges on this idea, and since such a notion of satisfaction and punishment is incompatible with his soteriology,[43] which does not allow for human cooperative participation in Christ's satisfaction for sin, purgatory too must be rejected.

Classical Lutheranism has likewise objected to the traditional Catholic teaching on purgatory, and for similar reasons. Setting aside the rejection of practices associated with the doctrine of purgatory (e.g., requiem Masses, indulgences, et cetera), the Lutheran critique of purgatory primarily confronts the idea of a need for personal satisfaction for sins already forgiven. In the *Apology of the Augsburg Confession* Melanchthon writes:

> Still [Catholics] admit that satisfactions do not contribute to the remission of guilt, though they imagine that they do contribute to the redemption of purgatorial and other punishments. They teach that in the forgiveness of sin God remits the guilt, and yet, because

---

[42] John Calvin, *Institutes of the Christian Religion*, Library of Christian Classics, vols. 20–21 (Philadelphia: The Westminster Press, 1960), bk. 3, ch. 5, §6.

[43] And more generally most mainstream Protestant soteriologies.

it is fitting for divine righteousness to punish sin, he commutes the eternal punishment to a temporal one . . . This whole theory is a recent fiction, without authority either in the Scripture or in the ancient writers of the church.[44]

Additionally, he adds a few paragraphs later, "The death of Christ, furthermore, is a satisfaction not only for guilt but also for eternal death."[45] In other words, Christ's Passion and death not only won the forgiveness of guilt but also the remission of all debt to divine justice, expressed here in its maximum instantiation as eternal death.[46]

Rather than seeing personal sufferings and even the voluntary penances that follow the forgiveness of sins as satisfactions, Lutherans have viewed them instead as a continuation of the process of putting to death the old man to be born again in Christ. As the U.S. Catholic-Lutheran dialogue statement *The Hope of Eternal Life* expresses it, "What had been understood in a juridical model of punishment and satisfaction is reconceived in the model of ongoing death and resurrection."[47] In this way man is thought to be progressively regenerated through the afflictions of daily life. Finally, this process is completed at the moment of death. As Luther's *Large Catechism* explains, "All this, then, is the office and work of the Holy Spirit, to begin and daily increase holiness on earth . . . Then, when we pass from this life, he will instantly perfect our holiness and will eternally preserve us in it."[48] Whatever transformation or purification is needed is thus completed in man's final hour—"the old self is finally purged in the death of the body," and purgatory has no place in this process.[49]

Nevertheless, despite the consistent critique from traditional Protestant theologies,[50] it is worthwhile to note that there has been a significant increase

---

[44] Philip Melanchthon, *Apology of the Augsburg Confession*, in *Book of Concord*, trans. Theodore G. Tappert (Philadelphia: Muhlenberg Press, 1959), art. 12, nos. 118–19.

[45] Melanchthon, *Apology of the Augsburg Confession*, art. 12b, no. 43.

[46] Christ did indeed make perfect satisfaction for all sins. However, it remains to be articulated how man receives and shares in that satisfaction. The Catholic position, as we will see in chapter five, acknowledges the perfect satisfaction of Christ while also recognizing the way that each individual is called to cooperate personally with it.

[47] Lutheran-Catholic Dialogue, *The Hope of Eternal Life* (Washington, DC: USCCB, 2010), 184, accessed August 25, 2021, https://www.usccb.org/committees/ecumenical-interreligious-affairs/hope-eternal-life.

[48] Martin Luther, *Large Catechism*, in *Book of Concord*, trans. Theodore G. Tappert (Philadelphia: Muhlenberg Press, 1959), part II, art. III, no. 59.

[49] Lutheran-Catholic Dialogue, *The Hope of Eternal Life*, 186.

[50] See also the thirty-nine Articles of Religion of the Church of England. "Articles of Religion,"

in interest in purgatory in the Protestant theological world in recent times. The trend has one of its principal roots in the work of C. S. Lewis. His *Letters to Malcom: Chiefly on Prayer* is often quoted in this regard:

> Our souls *demand* Purgatory, don't they? Would it not break the heart if God said to us, "It is true, my son, that your breath smells and your rags drip with mud and slime, but we are charitable here and no one will upbraid you with these things, nor draw away from you. Enter into the joy."? Should we not reply, "With submission, sir, and if there is no objection, I'd *rather* be cleaned first." "It may hurt, you know"—"Even so, sir."[51]

Since then a number of theologians, particularly those with philosophical interest, have taken up the theme and sought to present purgatory in a way that would be compatible with their greater soteriological concerns. David Brown's 1985 article "No Heaven without Purgatory" was seminal in this regard.[52] Since then, several other articles and publications have followed,[53] but particularly important was Jerry Walls's book *Purgatory: The Logic of Total Transformation*.[54] Walls's work represents a high-water mark to date in the Protestant theology of purgatory. He critically evaluates some of the recent work in the field and helpfully signals the various options and principles at stake. His work, like that of his contemporaries, is also consciously ecumenical. Walls and others have taken important steps to articulate the relevant issues that might distinguish a Protestant theology of purgatory from the Catholic version. Some, like Neal Judisch, have attempted to align the two doctrines, while others, like Justin D. Barnard, have emphasized their incompatibility. Happily, however, as is perhaps inevitable when discussing

---

Anglicans Online, updated May 23, 2017, http://anglicansonline.org/basics/thirty-nine_articles.html.

[51] C. S. Lewis, *Letters to Malcolm: Chiefly on Prayer* (London: Geoffrey Bles, 1964), 140.

[52] David Brown, "No Heaven without Purgatory," *Religious Studies* 21, no. 4 (December 1985): 447–56.

[53] Justin D. Barnard, "Purgatory and the Dilemma of Sanctification," *Faith and Philosophy* 24, no. 3 (July 2007): 311–30; David Vander Laan, "The Sanctification Argument for Purgatory," *Faith and Philosophy* 24, no. 3 (July 2007): 331–39; Neal Judisch, "Sanctification, Satisfaction, and the Purpose of Purgatory," *Faith and Philosophy* 26, no. 2 (April 2009): 167–85; Jerry L. Walls, *Heaven, Hell, and Purgatory: Rethinking the Things That Matter Most* (Grand Rapids, MI: Brazos Press, 2015); Kristof K. P. Vanhoutte and Benjamin McCraw, eds., *Purgatory: Philosophical Dimensions* (Cham, Switzerland: Palgrave Macmillan, 2017).

[54] Jerry L. Walls, *Purgatory: The Logic of Total Transformation* (New York: Oxford University Press, 2012).

this topic, all are attempting to do theology with an active awareness of the Catholic counterpart. Needless to say, engaging with this group of Protestant theologians on this topic should be an important part of the Catholic ecumenical project.

Nevertheless, Calvin's and Melanchthon's concerns have not gone away. Protestant arguments in favor of purgatory are not based on the demands of divine justice and do not include a notion of satisfaction. They typically focus exclusively on the soul's need for healing. In other words, they, like the Orthodox, agree with the second of our objects of purgatorial purification, the residual evil dispositions, but not with our third, the debt of punishment to be satisfied before God. In this line Barnard contrasts what he calls the "Satisfaction Model" (Catholic) and the "Sanctification Model" (Protestant):

> The suggestion that additional satisfaction for sin must be made by sinners themselves in purgatory undermines the sufficiency of Christ's work as a satisfaction for sin. . . . On the *Satisfaction Model*, what gets purged through the purgatorial process is the penalty for sin or sin itself. By contrast, what gets purged in the *Sanctification Model* is the disposition to sin. For Protestants, the possession of saving faith is sufficient for having sin or the penalty of sin 'purged' by virtue of Christ's work as a satisfaction for sin. Yet, the disposition to sin remains until the process of sanctification is complete.[55]

If there is any sense in which the soul in purgatory must still be punished for its sins, then Christ's salvation is ineffective, so the argument goes. Like for the Orthodox, the idea that freedom from guilt and freedom from punishment could be distinct seems irrational. "For, once guilt has been acknowledged, it is impossible to see what further purpose could be served in exacting punishment."[56]

Rather, for these Protestant proponents of purgatory, the raison d'être of purgatory is the necessity of the healing process, "process" being the key word, since this is the very reason they argue in favor of purgatory. All Protestants would agree that the souls in heaven are holy and thus do not sin; that is, they are morally perfect. However, there is an issue. As Barnard explains, "According to traditional Protestant theology, the possession of saving faith is a sufficient condition for enjoying eternal union and fellowship

---

[55] Barnard, "Dilemma of Sanctification," 326.
[56] Brown, "No Heaven without Purgatory," 456.

with God in heaven."[57] Nevertheless, "the possession of saving faith does not, by itself, entail that one possesses a morally sanctified nature."[58] In other words, there is a real, and often temporal, distinction between the possession of faith by which one will be saved and the moral perfection that the souls in heaven will have attained. Barnard precisely recognizes that it is also not enough to simply say that the souls in heaven de facto do not sin. Rather, they must have reached a point in their moral development by which they have become the kind of people who would not sin. To put it simply, they must have become truly holy. However, on earth many who have genuine saving faith are still the kind of people who would sin or who do sin. These two groups he refers to as the "sanctified" and the "lapsable."[59] "It is this sanctified nature that distinguishes those who no longer commit sinful acts *because they are sanctified* from those who no longer commit sinful acts merely because they are lucky. Thus, it seems plausible to suggest that *the Sanctified* possess a certain kind of settled virtuous disposition that *the Lapsable* lack."[60] For heaven to genuinely be a place of moral perfection, all the souls there must have become "sanctified."

This distinction, he argues, ought to be accepted by all Protestants. It is inevitable that such a transition must take place. Where the proponents of purgatory distinguish themselves is in arguing that it does not make sense for this transition to take place instantaneously at death (as Luther had claimed). They reject the view that Barnard calls "provisionism" by which God unilaterally supplies the settled virtuous disposition at the moment of death.[61] This was the great insight of Brown that inspired these theologians.

---

[57] Barnard, "Dilemma of Sanctification," 314.

[58] Barnard, "Dilemma of Sanctification," 314.

[59] Barnard, "Dilemma of Sanctification," 314–15.

[60] Barnard, "Dilemma of Sanctification," 315.

[61] Barnard, "Dilemma of Sanctification," 317. This is the view eloquently advocated by the famous American revivalist Jonathan Edwards. It is interesting to note the similarity between this view and that of Bellarmine and Suarez. Edwards writes, "At death the believer . . . is adorned with a perfect and glorious holiness; the work of sanctification is then completed and the beautiful image of God has then its finishing strokes by the pencil of God, and begins to shine forth with a heavenly beauty like a seraphim: then that grace which was so suppressed and kept under by the devil and the remainders of corruption, begins to find itself at liberty, breaks out and flames forth into pure flames, and the soul begins to shine like the brightness of the firmament." Jonathan Edwards, "Sermons and Discourses 1720–1723 (WJE Online Vol. 10)," ed. Wilson H. Kimnach, Jonathan Edwards Center at Yale University, accessed January 11, 2020, http://edwards.yale.edu/archive/?path=aHR0cDovL2Vkd2FyZHMueWFsZS5lZHUvY2dpLWJpb i9uZXdwaGlsby9nZXRvYmplY3QucGw/Yy45OjQ6MDowOjU2LndqZW8uODI4MDk4 LjgyODEwMS44MjgxMDcuODI4MTEx.

As Brown writes, "there is no way of rendering such an abrupt transition in essentially temporal beings conceivable."[62] His arguments are primarily philosophical and based upon psychological conceptions of personal continuity, but all versions of the contemporary Protestant defense of purgatory revolve around at least some kind of unfittingness of such an instantaneous transition. God either cannot or will not do it. Barnard summarizes his own argument by saying:

> to the extent that death does represent an arbitrary point in the process of sanctification, any reason that would justify God in making unilateral provisions for *the Lapsable* to become *the Sanctified* at death ought to justify God in making such provisions now. Moreover, any significant good that would be sacrificed by God's provision now, would seemingly be sacrificed by God's provision at one's death. If there is no significant good that would be sacrificed by God's provision now, then God's failure to avail himself of the option of perfecting *the Lapsable* seemingly makes him morally culpable for the evil that results from their actions.[63]

In other words, although God could have immediately sanctified us the moment we first began to possess saving faith, there clearly must be some good obtained by not doing so, a good so great that it justifies his permission of the many evils that result from our remaining with a "lapsable" nature. That good, Barnard argues, is the process of sanctification itself.[64] It is simply good that man undergo this progressive move from a lapsable to a sanctified nature. It is good that it takes time. Barnard, however, does not develop this point at length. He does not explain *why* that process is so great a good. It is simply the only explanation that makes sense of God's activity. It must be the case, he says, that God's unilateral action "would compromise the overriding value of the internal integrity of the process itself."[65]

Similarly, Barnard sees no reason why God's motivation or activity would change at the moment of death. Death, he suggests, is an arbitrary point along the process of sanctification. There is no real connection, in other words, between the physical process of dying per se and the spiritual process of sanctification. Being sanctified does not lead to dying or dying

---

[62] Brown, "No Heaven without Purgatory," 16.
[63] Barnard, "Dilemma of Sanctification," 325.
[64] Barnard, "Dilemma of Sanctification," 327.
[65] Barnard, "Dilemma of Sanctification," 327.

to sanctification (spiritual metaphors aside), strictly speaking. Hence, why should God's activity toward the soul in that process change at a relatively arbitrary point? Would not the good of the internal integrity of the process remain after death as much as before?

Of course, Catholics can rightly object that the doctrines of the particular judgment and the moment of death as the end of merit mean that death is not simply an arbitrary point. Rather, death is a key moment at which God's activity toward the soul does change for important reasons. As I will argue in the third chapter, Barnard's identification of the good of the transformative process is a welcome point. Aquinas himself points to the providential reasons for the overall good of a given person to explain why God does not completely remove all of the penalties of sin at the moment of baptism.[66] Fighting to overcome such defects can actually redound to the soul's glory. However, these reasons no longer apply to the soul in the same way when the opportunity for merit has ended. Then, so I will argue, the satisfaction of the *reatus poenae* remains the only sufficiently good reason why God does not immediately heal the soul's dispositional imperfections. For the reasons already identified, however, satisfaction of the *reatus poenae* is a good that Barnard cannot acknowledge.

In response to Barnard, Judisch argued that, if properly understood, there is actually no difference between the "Satisfaction" and "Sanctification" models. Although himself a Protestant, he argues that the true Catholic position is that satisfaction is nothing other than enduring the process of healing:

> Rather, the consequence of sin which issues in "temporal punishment" is identical to the *corrosive effect of sin itself* upon the individual's soul; the "temporal punishment" of this consequence, accordingly, consists in the individual's *enduring through* and *struggling to rectify* the *disorder of his soul* and *spiritual health* that sinful behavior brings in its wake; and finally, "making satisfaction" for sins, in this context, is to be understood as the individual's *doing whatever is required* (and allowing God to do *to* him whatever's required) to *restore his spiritual well-being* and so to be *"purged"* *of his self-destructive attachment* to sin. To put it another way, sin-fulness—the self-reinforcing urge to commit iniquity introduced through original sin and fostered by the habitual exercise of our capacity for it, or what the tradition calls "concupiscence"—*just is* the second consequence of sin, the "temporal punishment" for

---

[66] *ST* IIIa, q. 69, a. 3.

which sinners must suffer here or in purgatory. It is not some additional "judicial" penalty God imposes on sinners from on high with the expectation of their finding a way, somehow or other, to "make satisfaction" in the form of "payment" for their debts; it is as it were, the "natural" punishment sin itself brings upon those who commit it, rather as virtue is said to bring its own reward.[67]

His presentation here is certainly one of the best ecumenical attempts at uniting Catholic and Protestant visions of purgatory. It also sounds remarkably similar to the position of Ware presented above. If his account is accurate, then the ecumenical fruit in the East and the West would be significant, and, in many ways, it does seem like he is on the right track. We could say that he is attempting to unite our second and third categories from above—evil dispositions and the debt of punishment before God. Nevertheless, while I do think his suggestion promises a way forward, it is not quite as theologically innocent as it seems. In this book, I too am arguing that the punishment endured by the souls in purgatory should be seen in its intimate connection to the process of internal transformation. It is a medicinal punishment, and so the two aspects are harmonious. Nevertheless, they cannot be reduced to one another. Not just any process of transformation will do for a Catholic account of purgatory, but only one that retains a punitive modality in accordance with the requirements of divine justice. As a fuller explanation of the *reatus poenae* will show and as the presentation of Aquinas's position in the first chapter has already suggested, the Catholic position must account for the fundamental irreducibility of the punishment owed to divine justice and of subjective interior transformation, even as it maintains the harmony of the two.

In his book, Walls acknowledges this point. He argues that the position of Catholics, such as Aquinas, should be called the Satisfaction/Sanctification Model.[68] Emphases on the two aspects can certainly fluctuate. Nevertheless, no matter how similar contemporary versions of Catholic and Protestant images of purification may appear, if Aquinas and Catholics with him ultimately insist that in some sense personal satisfaction is owed to divine justice, there can be no strict identity between the two models. In this case we arrive back at the same Orthodox and Protestant concerns presented in these two sections. In the end, then, the debate hinges on the idea of the *reatus poenae* and its satisfaction.

---

[67] Judisch, "Purpose of Purgatory," 176.
[68] Walls, *Logic of Total Transformation*, 71.

Conclusion

From what has been presented above, it is clear that the central issue of purgatory is the notion of punishment and the *reatus poenae*. For the Catholics—Scotus, Bellarmine, and Suarez—this debt of punishment is the principal (and potentially exclusive) object of purification in purgatory. In the position proposed by Bellarmine, for example, the other objects are addressed somewhat instantaneously and only the *reatus poenae* is purified in purgatory.[69] For Scotus, the remission of sins is simply subsumed into the punishment. For the opponents of the Catholic position, including both those who do and do not believe in some form of purgatory, the satisfaction of the debt of punishment forms the chief point of contention with the traditional Catholic doctrine. Every debate revolves around this issue. Even this circumstantial evidence, then, should be enough to suggest that we have discovered the heart of the matter.

Enough was said above to recognize that there is a significant fundamental agreement between Bellarmine, Suarez, and Aquinas. The scriptural and magisterial teachings which follow in the next chapter do not challenge their positions in any significant way. Adequate adjudication concerning their doctrines can only be conducted after a more thorough look at Aquinas's own position. However, some important topics should be examined based on the ideas of Scotus, the Orthodox, and the Protestants. Their positions presented here, I will argue, are not consistent with the faith of the Church for important reasons.

In particular, the theory suggested by Scotus and the teaching of these non-Catholics make a similar but contrary point. Neither admits the possibility of punishment remaining after the forgiveness of sin. For Scotus, the fulfillment of the punishment is the forgiveness, so if forgiveness is obtained that is because, in some way, the *reatus poenae* has been satisfied. For the Orthodox and Protestants, in general terms, Christ has completely satisfied for sins, and the individual believer has no part to play in that process. Hence, if one is truly forgiven then the punishment is also completely removed. Neither position sees the possible concurrence of genuine restored innocence and punishment. In other words, neither can grasp the place of punishment *within* a relationship of friendship with God.

In contrast, by maintaining the distinction between moral innocence, internal transformation, and the demands of divine justice, Aquinas's system

---

[69] I have not yet presented it here, but Aquinas, Bellarmine, and Suarez all teach that venial sins are remitted by a single act of charity in the first moment after death. We will see this doctrine in more detail in chapter four.

is able to account more faithfully for the transformative power of a divinely imposed punishment within our relationship with God. That relationship is not reduced to a purely external measure of divine justice in a kind of arbitrary or voluntaristic way, as it is in the position suggested by Scotus. Neither, however, does it abandon such objective measures in favor of an exclusively personal and subjective account, as for the Orthodox and the Protestants. It is with Aquinas, then, that we are truly able to see both the irreducibility and the harmony of these two dimensions. He gives us a vision of our relationship with God in which forgiveness is the foundation and beginning of a process that simultaneously heals us internally of all the inherent consequences of sin and also makes due reparation and satisfaction in a way that accords with the objective demands of divine justice. This, so I will argue in the following two chapters, is the essential foundation for understanding the true nature of purgatory.

CHAPTER III

Punishment and the *Reatus Poenae*

THE PREVIOUS TWO CHAPTERS have made it clear that a proper under-standing of punishment and the *reatus poenae* is at the heart of the question of purgatory. In the first chapter I showed that Aquinas identified the *reatus poenae* as one of the essential and irreducible objects of purification after death. In the second chapter we saw that it is a central idea for the Catholic defenders of purgatory and that the key debates concerning purgatory between Catholics and the Orthodox and Protestants have all centered around this issue. Nevertheless, although we have seen that Aquinas main-tains the existence of the *reatus poenae* distinct from guilt or the residual evil dispositions left by sin, I have not yet shown how Aquinas defends this position. Such is the task of this chapter.

However, given the controversial nature of this topic (especially in contemporary times), it is helpful to see before examining Aquinas's own treatment what scriptural and magisterial support his position has. This brief turn to the authorities, though, is not meant to evade the need for rigorous theological reasoning. Rather, in typical Thomistic fashion, a survey of these sources of theology is meant to ensure that our investigation is headed in the right direction. If it cannot first be shown that the teaching of Aquinas has its roots in divine revelation itself, then our analysis of his theology would only be of historical interest. It is my claim that Aquinas's explanation has perennial value for the Church and is a crucial aid for a full understanding of purgatory today. To say this, however, we must be sure that his argument is compatible with an honest reading of Sacred Scripture and the Church's teaching.

Guided by the analysis of the various positions at the end of the last chap-ter, we will look in particular for examples of divine punishment exercised after the forgiveness of sins. There are certainly opponents of the idea that God punishes at all, but if it can be shown that the idea that God punishes even after he has forgiven someone's sins can be found in Scripture, then the broader position is thereby demonstrated as well. In reality, though, it is the more restricted claim—punishment after forgiveness—that nearly all opponents of the Catholic doctrine on purgatory reject. This, then, is the key point of debate and the object of our inquiry. Nevertheless, while focusing predominantly on the punitive reality, we should not fail to notice the internal healing that accompanies it. This will aid us in the next chapter to understand more deeply the medicinal nature of purgatorial punishments which I will there attempt to defend.

Scripture

It does not take long to see that the Scriptures do suggest that there are times when God punishes after having forgiven a sin. In several key passages we see this dynamic unfold. I will include only a few of the most poignant examples here, but the pattern will become clear. One of the earliest cases is found with the Israelites in the desert in the book of Numbers. The people lament and murmur against Moses and Aaron after Caleb and the others had surveyed the promised land. After hearing the report about the other inhabitants, the chosen people do not have confidence that the Lord can secure the land for them. God appears and threatens to disinherit the people and make of Moses "a nation greater and mightier than they."[1] Moses, however, intercedes and obtains reconciliation for the people:

> "And now, I beg you, let the power of the Lord be great as you have promised, saying, 'The Lord is slow to anger, and abounding in mercy, forgiving iniquity and transgression, but he will by no means clear the guilty, visiting the iniquity of fathers upon children, upon the third and upon the fourth generation.' Pardon the iniquity of this people, I beg you, according to the greatness of your mercy, and according as you have forgiven this people, from Egypt even until now." Then the Lord said, "*I have pardoned*, according to your word; but truly, as I live, and as all the earth shall be filled with the glory of the Lord, none of the men who have seen my glory and my signs which I wrought in Egypt and in the wilderness, and yet have put me to the proof these ten times and have not hearkened to my voice, shall see the land which I swore to give to their fathers; and none of those who despised me shall see it."[2]

---

[1] Num 14:12.

[2] Num 14:19–23 (emphasis mine).

The plea for pardon is granted. The people are forgiven, but punishment still follows. They are not disinherited, but none of them will enter the promised land.

In his analysis of this passage Jacob Milgrom focuses heavily on the meaning of the word translated here as "pardon," in Hebrew, *salaḥ*.[3] *Salaḥ*, so he argues, "indicates [God's] desire for reconciliation with man in order to continue His relationship with him—in Israelite terms, to maintain His covenant."[4] It is something that only God can provide—only God is the subject of *salaḥ*. Similarly, the Hebrew word bears a semantic relationship with the Akkadian *salāḥu*, a verb meaning "asperse" and connected to rituals of healing. By *salaḥ*, God thus reestablishes his covenantal commitment to his people. *Salaḥ* does not, however, indicate forgiveness or pardon by a kind of complete exoneration that would cancel all punishment.[5] Rather, as Milgrom explains, "Moses is quite content to invoke the dreaded doctrine of vertical retribution [punishment on successive generations], provided that *salaḥ* will also be dispensed, justice will be tempered by mercy, and God will continue as Israel's God and fulfill the promise of his covenant."[6] The fact that God does grant Moses's request—"*salaḥti,* as you have asked"—while still inflicting the punishment of a lengthy sojourn in the desert shows that the restoration of divine friendship (forgiveness) and a protracted punishment are compatible.

Another similar example is found in the account of the sin of David with Bathsheba. When the prophet Nathan confronts David about his sin,

---

3 Jacob Milgrom, *Numbers*, JPS Torah Commentary Series (Philadelphia: Jewish Publication Society, 1989), 112, 392–96.

4 Milgrom, *Numbers*, 396.

5 Admittedly, Milgrom explicitly argues that *salah* cannot mean forgiveness. While, at face value, this affirmation runs contrary to the position that I am using Milgrom to support, it becomes clear that the disagreement is merely verbal. Forgiveness, pardon, or the absolution of sin, for Milgrom and the sources he relies upon, mean such a complete eradication of sin that no divine retributive punishment will follow. He quotes from Ibn Ezra, who states, "Since we have the verse 'they shall not see the land' (14:20) after God said 'I pardoned, as you asked' (v. 20) we know that the expression *selah na*', 'pardon, I pray' (v. 19), [is a prayer that God be] long-suffering [to them but not that they be forgiven]." *Numbers*, 393. However, to presuppose that forgiveness necessarily includes a remission of all punishment would be begging the question in the context of the current discussion. Forgiveness, as I am using the term, need not necessarily include this latter element. At times God does mercifully act in this way, but that does not mean that true forgiveness is limited to those occasions. In any case, Milgrom shows that in the passage from Numbers what is given by God is a merciful restoration of the covenantal relationship that, nevertheless, still includes an element of divine retributive punishment. This, so I argue, is sufficient to call it forgiveness.

6 Milgrom, *Numbers*, 396.

David eventually confesses: "I have sinned against the Lord."[7] Clearly, he is contrite, for we see that God forgives him his sin, but punishment still follows. The text continues, "Nathan said to David, '*The Lord also has put away your sin*; you shall not die. Nevertheless, because by this deed you have utterly scorned the Lord, the child that is born to you shall die.'"[8] This passage is particularly lucid because of the unambiguous statement that the Lord had "put away his sin." Nevertheless, a punishment does follow. As P. Kyle McCarter Jr. explains, "The sin cannot simply be forgotten: It must be atoned for. Thus, if David himself is not to die, the sin must be transferred to someone who will."[9]

Furthermore, we can note that the punishment is strikingly distinct from the automatic and direct consequence of the sin. Naturally and directly, the sinful act led to the procreation of the child. However, insofar as it was an offense to God's justice, it led dispositively to the child's death. It is a stark example but is helpful for its clarity. Here, in particular, we can also note the apparent medicinal finality of the punishment. By conceding to the divine decree in fasting, prayer, and trusting surrender, David is internally transformed. By God's providential guidance, David accepts his suffering as a part of the order of divine justice and consequently as an opportunity for conversion in such a way that he himself is also more deeply perfected.

The medicinal element is even more evident, as we should expect, in the New Testament, and yet the teaching remains the same. The most evident example is found in the twelfth chapter of the book of Hebrews. There we read, "My son, do not regard lightly the discipline of the Lord, nor lose courage when you are punished by him. For the Lord disciplines him whom he loves, and chastises every son whom he receives."[10] The Lord loves and receives his children by mercifully forgiving their sins, and yet they must still endure a fitting discipline and chastisement. A similar teaching is given by our Lord himself in Revelation. Jesus tells the Church in Laodicea, "Those whom I love, I reprove and chasten; so be zealous and repent."[11] Here again we are taught that, even within a relationship of love and forgiveness, the sinner must bear his proper punishment.

Thus too, in conclusion, understood Zachaeus who, upon meeting Christ, offered to give half his money to the poor and to pay back fourfold

---

[7]   2 Sam 12:13.

[8]   2 Sam 12:13–14 (emphasis mine).

[9]   P. Kyle McCarter Jr., *II Samuel*, Anchor Bible Series (Garden City, NY: Doubleday & Company, Inc., 1984), 301.

[10]   Heb 12:5b–6.

[11]   Rev 3:19.

those whom he had wronged, far exceeding the minimal demands of restitution.[12] In doing this he willingly embraces the principles of retributive justice as taught in the Law.[13] As Exodus 22:1 states, "he shall pay . . . four sheep for a [stolen] sheep."[14] This fourfold repayment recognizes a higher justice, one that includes making reparation for misdeeds rather than simply settling accounts.

Importantly, too, although Zacchaeus promised to perform these actions before he received forgiveness, he would only have completed them afterwards. Jesus does not, then, correct him and say, "Thank you for the offer, but rely not on your own works; I forgive you and alone will make satisfaction in your place." Rather, by his silence we are led to believe that he approved of Zacchaeus's proposal. Our Lord recognized his zeal for divine justice in the midst of his conversion. Thus, in this passage as in the others we see yet again an irreducible element of punitive satisfaction. Certainly, it is incorporated within a dynamic of forgiveness and healing, but it cannot be simply subsumed into either. Many passages of Scripture thus support this notion of the importance and significance of punishment within a plenary reconciliation of the sinner with a loving and merciful God.

Admittedly, however, no single Scripture passage or collection of them confirms our reading beyond all possible argument. There will always be those who disagree, and we cannot presume that our interlocutors were unaware of these passages and this reading of the texts. Although a clear picture does emerge when we view them together, it is always essential to return to the teaching of the Church and theological reflection to guide our interpretation of the Scriptures.

Magisterium

At important points in her history the Church has had to clarify the issue of punishment for sin, and hence there is not a lack of reference to the *reatus poenae* and its satisfaction in official proclamations. The decree from the Council of Florence that followed the debates with Mark of Ephesus is one such example. The Council stated that "if those who are truly penitent die in the love of God before having satisfied by worthy fruits of penance for their sins of commission and omission, their souls are cleansed after death

---

[12] Luke 19:1–10.

[13] Joseph A. Fitzmyer, *The Gospel According to Luke (X–XXIV)*, Anchor Bible Series (Garden City, NY: Doubleday & Company, Inc., 1985), 1225.

[14] Exodus 22:1i; cf. 2 Sam 12:6.

by purgatorial punishments."[15] Especially in the context of the preceding debates, the reference to satisfaction and punishment clearly refers to this debt owed to divine justice. Mark's refusal to sign the document is a further confirmation of this interpretation.

Additionally, while our investigation focuses on purgatory, there is also an overlap with the sacrament of penance. At times, clear articulation of a certain idea relevant to purgatory is found in the Church's exposition of this sacrament of healing. This is certainly the case with the expiation of the debt of punishment after death, since the same logic is also behind the imposition of a penance after the confession of sin. Both are forms of satisfaction. Hence the Council of Trent declared that "if anyone says that the whole punishment is always remitted by God together with the guilt and that the satisfaction of penitents is nothing else but the faith by which they realize that Christ has satisfied for them, let him be anathema."[16] Again, the element of satisfaction, now articulated in conscious contrast to the Protestant position, makes it clear that the Council is speaking about an obligation before God remaining after forgiveness.

This teaching has also been articulated more recently in contemporary times. In the Apostolic Constitution *Indulgentiarum Doctrina* St. Paul VI taught that "it is a divinely revealed truth that sins bring punishments inflicted by God's sanctity and justice."[17] He continues, "that punishment or the vestiges of sin may remain to be expiated or cleansed and that they in fact frequently do even after the remission of guilt is clearly demonstrated by the doctrine on purgatory."[18] Finally, the *Catechism of the Catholic Church*, in unison with him, also teaches that "the forgiveness of sin and restoration of communion with God entail the remission of the eternal punishment of sin, but temporal punishment of sin remains."[19] Thus, successive generations of authority in the Church have unambiguously taught that there is a punishment for sin that remains even after forgiveness.

---

[15] Denzinger, *Compendium*, §1304: "si vere paenitentes in Dei caritate decesserint, antequam dignis paenitentiae fructibus de commissis satisfecerint et omissis, eorum animas poenis purgatoriis post mortem purgari."

[16] Denzinger, *Compendium*, §1712: "si quis dixerit, totam poenam simul cum culpa remitti semper a Deo, satisfactionemque paenitentium non esse aliam quam fidem, qua apprehendunt Christum pro eis satisfecisse: anathema sit."

[17] Paul VI, Apostolic Constitution *Indulgentiarum Doctrina* (January 1, 1967), 2, as published in Apostolic Penitentiary, *Manual of Indulgences: Norms and Grants* (Washington, DC: USCCB, 1999).

[18] Paul VI, *Indulgentiarum Doctrina*, 3. This is the actually the clearest rejection of the Scotist position.

[19] CCC, §1473.

Our investigation of the Church's teaching then supports what we encountered in the Scriptures and points us toward the distinction between guilt, evil dispositions, and the *reatus poenae* as suggested by Aquinas. Divine revelation and the teaching of the Church have given us considerable reasons to follow this line of understanding. God's providential care of man, so we saw, has wisely ordained that punishment follows upon sin, even after forgiveness. Even though in numerous examples it is incorporated within a dynamic of healing and transformation, it cannot simply be reduced to those elements. It is something unique with its own logic.

Nevertheless, it could still be objected that the term "punishment" is analogous. We have already seen that Aquinas himself makes this point. At times the inherent consequences of sin are called "temporal punishment." Judisch, as we saw in chapter two, uses this analogical understanding of punishment and his reading of the Church's documents to do away with the distinction between the *reatus poenae* and the immanent consequences of sin. If "punishment" is flexible, why cannot "satisfaction" and all other related terms be as well? "Satisfaction" is a restoration of justice, granted, but is not the most important justice the proper ordering of one's own soul, one's inner life? The objection is significant and cannot be dismissively rejected. Nevertheless, the presentation of Aquinas's punitive theory that follows explains why such a reading is not permitted. There is an analogy, but every analogy includes both similarity and *dissimilarity*. Thus, as we will see, although the analogical use of "punishment" is helpful and illuminative, it does not allow us to conflate the two forms of "punishment" as Judisch and others have attempted.

THOMISTIC PUNITIVE THEORY

Interestingly, Aquinas's most systematic presentation of his punitive theory is found in the *Summa* precisely in his explanation of the *reatus poenae* as a consequence of sin. Thus, his understanding of punishment, while being broad enough to adequately account for all of its various expressions, never loses the divine perspective and its reference to God's justice. His explanation is as follows:

> I answer that it has passed from natural things to human affairs that whenever one thing rises up against another, it suffers some detriment therefrom.... Wherefore we find that the natural inclination of man is to repress those who rise up against him. Now it is evident that all things contained in an order, are, in a manner, one,

57

in relation to the principle of that order. Consequently, whatever rises up against an order, is put down by that order or by the principle thereof. And because sin is an inordinate act, it is evident that whoever sins, commits an offense against an order: wherefore he is put down, in consequence, by that same order, which repression is punishment.[20]

Every ordered whole, he explains, from the most elementary being to the entire divinely ordered cosmos, represses whatever acts contrary to it either in virtue of the order itself or by the principle of the order. Inanimate objects, men, and God all act this way, though each in accordance with its nature, that is, analogously. In human society this tendency is principally expressed by the state in its punishment of criminals. More fundamentally, however, it is ingrained in every individual as a natural inclination of the human will. Man is naturally drawn to repress those who act against him. The passion of anger is the innate, affective expression of that inclination.[21] It is the movement of the sensitive appetite that "essentially desires the punishment of someone perceived to be a wrongdoer."[22] It is a passion common to human experience.

Further, as we saw above, it is a basic principle of Thomistic anthropology and morality that human inclinations are naturally good. They are ordered by God the Creator in accordance with the good of human nature. Admittedly, such an orientation to the good is *diminished* by original sin, as we have seen, but diminished does not mean destroyed. Although in our fallen state we can and should question many of the expressions of anger and the desire for the repression of wrongdoers, we cannot devalue the basic orientation. Since it is rooted in a natural human inclination, it is fundamentally good and leads us to the good: namely, the repression of the one acting against the unifying order. When this takes place amongst moral agents the repression is properly called punishment.

In the current context of moral philosophy, however, it is not enough

---

[20] *ST* Ia-IIae, q. 87, a. 1: "Respondeo dicendum quod ex rebus naturalibus ad res humanas derivatur ut id quod contra aliquid insurgit, ab eo detrimentum patiatur. . . . Unde in hominibus hoc ex naturali inclinatione invenitur, ut unusquisque deprimat eum qui contra ipsum insurgit. Manifestum est autem quod quaecumque continentur sub aliquo ordine, sunt quodammodo unum in ordine ad principium ordinis. Unde quidquid contra ordinem aliquem insurgit, consequens est ut ab ipso ordine, vel principe ordinis, deprimatur. Cum autem peccatum sit actus inordinatus, manifestum est quod quicumque peccat, contra aliquem ordinem agit. Et ideo ab ipso ordine consequens est quod deprimatur. Quae quidem depressio poena est."

[21] *ST* II-IIae, q. 158, a. 1.

[22] Peter Karl Koritansky, *Thomas Aquinas and the Philosophy of Punishment* (Washington, DC: The Catholic University of America Press, 2012), 118.

simply to point to the natural inclination. Many are suspicious of inclinations and in speaking of divine punishment suspect natural law theorists of projecting arbitrary or perverse human desires onto our conceptions of right and wrong. We can understand Aquinas's reasons and the anthropology, but it is not as easily accepted today. Such an account presupposes a particular anthropology which is no longer predominant, owing in particular to the influence of Immanuel Kant. Jeremy Bentham, for instance, remarked, "A great multitude of people are continually talking of the law of nature; and when they give you their sentiments about what is right and what is wrong you are to understand that these sentiments are so many chapters and sections of the law of nature."[23] "In what way can these 'sentiments' really be the grounding of a moral philosophy?" he would have us ask.

Even faithful Catholics should have appropriate concerns about an overly simplistic application of Aquinas's natural law argument like the one Bentham caricatures. In a world so obviously broken, can we really trust natural inclination as an appropriate guide for morality? When speaking about supposedly just, punitive retribution there seems to be a real threat of falling into such a moralistic projection of our desires. Many trace man's desire for punishment not to a good natural inclination ingrained in nature by God but to a perverse proclivity for inflicting harm. They imagine something closer to Nietzsche's disturbing affirmation: "This world," he writes, "has never really lost a certain savour of blood and torture. . . . Because the *infliction* of suffering produces the highest degree of happiness. . . . Without cruelty, no feast: so teaches the oldest and longest history of man—and in punishment too is there so much of the *festive*."[24] In the contemporary mind, the step from Aquinas to Nietzsche on this point does not seem so exaggerated. Thus, if we are going to rely on an argument for divine punishment from natural human inclination, we must reinforce the foundation of a proper understanding of human nature.

We should note that Bentham fails to distinguish between authentic natural inclinations and any given human desire, no matter how corrupt it may have become. There is a world of difference, however, between "sentiment," as Bentham uses the term, and Aquinas's understanding of inclination. In

---

[23] Jeremy Bentham, *An Introduction to the Principles of Morals and Legislation*, ed. Jonathan Bennett, Early Modern Texts (2017), 16, accessed March 7, 2020, https://www.earlymoderntexts.com/assets/pdfs/bentham1780.pdf.

[24] Friedrich Nietzsche, *The Genealogy of Morals,* trans. Horace B. Samuel (London: T.N. Foulis, 1913), essay 2, §6, pp. 72–75, accessed March 7, 2020, https://www.gutenberg.org/files/52319/52319-h/52319-h.htm.

the first place, natural inclinations flow directly from the natural form.[25] A thing's basic inclinations necessarily result from what it is. This is true from the simplest elemental particle to the most complex life form. Furthermore, the natural form which produces these inclinations is given by God. Thus, the form and the inclinations that flow from it are naturally good and are a kind of participation in the wisdom of the Creator.

One obvious and relevant example is the inclination to self-preservation. All things, in accordance with their nature, are inclined to self-preservation. Fire consumes more and more wood; seals avoid sharks. Such is the nature of the world. In man, however, the situation is more complex because we possess a higher and more sophisticated nature. Man is inclined toward his good at various levels. Inasmuch as he is a being, he is inclined to self-preservation. Inasmuch as he is an animal, that inclination is expressed more profoundly through eating and procreation. These are still inherent to our nature, but here there is a more significant cognitive dimension involved. Finally, at his highest level, man is inclined to the good in itself through his rational appetite which we call the will.[26] It is a natural inclination, but without any particular given specification. It is man's freedom to identify and pursue the truly rational good in itself.

These distinct inclinations, however, ought to be viewed both concordantly and hierarchically, and not disjunctively. Man, for instance, shares the inclination to eating and procreation with all animals, but in him reason must order them to the highest end, the truly rational good, and not pursue them indiscriminately. When man pursues them rationally, eating becomes a meal and procreation a family. When he does not, they become gluttony and promiscuity. Nevertheless, no perversion takes away from the inherent goodness of the natural inclination. Eating is a good inclination even in a world of overweight people. Distortions of the inclination only underscore the importance of directing it in accordance with reason. Inclinations must simply be integrated, lived, and expressed in an authentically reasonable and human way in order for humans to reach the good to which nature inclines them.

The very same reasoning applies to the inclination to repress the one who contravenes the unifying order, which we have been discussing. It is an inclination that flows from nature and is shared by all things in some basic way. We could call it the combative or irascible half of the desire for self-preservation. Things not only desire what is good for them and reject

---

25 *ST* Ia, q. 80, a. 1.
26 *ST* Ia, q. 59, a. 1.

what is harmful but also actively resist obstacles and attacks. Hence "fire has a natural inclination, not only to rise from a lower position, which is unsuitable to it, toward a higher position which is suitable, but also to resist whatever destroys or hinders its action."[27] So explains Aquinas.

Further, as this argument has shown, since the inclination to repress the wrongdoer flows from our nature which comes from God, it must be good. It is ordered to the genuine flourishing of human nature. However, we must still clarify the exact nature of the good that is being pursued. On some basic level, as I have already suggested, it is a form of self-preservation. Nevertheless, in human life it also extends beyond that. Mankind is not simply a collection of isolated individuals but is social by nature,[28] and thus the inclination to repress the wrongdoer also has a fitting social expression. In the case of the individual, it appropriately expresses itself as self-defense, but in society it becomes punishment properly speaking. Punishment, in other words, is the expression of the same inclination, now not merely between individuals but between an individual and the social order taken as a whole. Just as every individual expresses this tendency given by God, so too does a social order.[29] This is because society possesses a unity that imitates the substantial unity of creatures—a unity which gives it its form and life. As Aquinas wrote in the passage we saw at the beginning of this section, "It is evident that all things contained in an order, are, in a manner, one, in relation to the principle of that order. Consequently, whatever rises up against an order, is put down by that order or by the principle thereof."[30] Thus, just as a man's individual self-defense represses the wrongdoer in order to preserve his own life (his personal principle of unity), so too by means of punishment does society seek to preserve its life, its principle of unity. The unity of society, however, is nothing other than the proper relations of the members to the whole; in short, justice.[31] Justice, we can say, is to society what life is to the creature.

---

[27] *ST* Ia, q. 81, a. 2: "ignis habet naturalem inclinationem non solum ut recedat ab inferiori loco, qui sibi non convenit, et tendat in locum superiorem sibi convenientem; sed etiam quod resistat corrumpentibus et impedientibus."

[28] *ST* Ia-IIae, q. 72, a. 4.

[29] A human society is under the same obligation as the individual to direct this inclination in accordance with reason. *Mutatis mutandis*, a comparison could be made between an unjust society which viciously oppresses peaceful dissidents and a criminal who attacks his arresting officer.

[30] *ST* Ia-IIae, q. 87, a. 1: "Manifestum est autem quod quaecumque continentur sub aliquo ordine, sunt quodammodo unum in ordine ad principium ordinis. Unde quidquid contra ordinem aliquem insurgit, consequens est ut ab ipso ordine, vel principe ordinis, deprimatur."

[31] *ST* IIa-IIae, q. 58, a. 5.

Punishment is therefore the means by which the equality of justice, and thereby the life of the society, is preserved in the face of the wrongdoer.[32]

Punishment accomplishes this goal because it restores the proper ordering to society. Aquinas explains this idea in the *Compendium theologiae*, saying, "Punishment . . . restores right order, because by sinning a man exceeds the limits of the natural order, bestowing upon his will more than is right. Hence a return to the order of justice is effected by punishment, whereby [something] is withdrawn from the sinner's will."[33] The very contrariness to the will, so this text explains, is the essence of punishment. As Peter Koritansky writes, "Punishment's contrariety to the will is necessary to answer the 'overindulgent' will of the criminal act. Because the essence of crime involves a transgression of the will by which someone voluntarily goes 'too far' in following his criminal intentions, the essence of punishment represses that will by inflicting some kind of harm upon the criminal."[34]

However, punishment is not simply about returning that person individually to his own proper ordering to society. It is not purely or exclusively about the rehabilitation of the criminal. Without excluding the good of the wrongdoer, it must be remembered that the justice sought is a truly social good. "What needs correcting, according to the above argument, is not the criminal's will itself," Koritansky clarifies, "but a certain kind of inequality that comes about as a result of the crime."[35] We can certainly hope that the punishment will rehabilitate and heal the wrongdoer (the best punishments aim to do this), but this is not the immediate scope of punishment per se.

Importantly, neither is the criminal's evil or suffering the direct object desired by punishment. This too would be too personal and particular of an aim. Hatred, properly speaking, is that which seeks the evil of the other. Righteous punishment, in contrast, aims at the good of justice. It is the quest for the truly social good of justice that properly distinguishes punishment. As Aquinas clarifies, "The hater wishes evil to his enemy, as evil, whereas the angry man wishes evil to him with whom he is angry, not as evil but insofar as he reckons it just."[36] In a way, then, both reform and harm are too

---

[32] *ST* IIa-IIae, q. 108, a. 4.

[33] *Compendium theologiae*, lib. 1, cap. 121: "Est etiam ordinativa ipsius, quia per culpam homo transgreditur metas ordinis naturalis, plus suae voluntati tribuens quam oportet; unde ad ordinem iustitiae fit reductio per poenam per quam subtrahitur aliquid voluntati."

[34] Koritansky, *Aquinas and the Philosophy of Punishment*, 124.

[35] Koritansky, *Aquinas and the Philosophy of Punishment*, 124.

[36] *ST* Ia-IIae, q 46, a. 6: "odiens appetit malum inimici, inquantum est malum; iratus autem appetit malum eius contra quem irascitur, non inquantum est malum, sed inquantum habet quandam rationem boni, scilicet prout aestimat illud esse iustum."

particular to be the true goal. Punishment is ultimately about the restoration of justice for society.

Different Modes of Punishment

Having thus clarified that punishment is the infliction of some evil against the will of the guilty for the sake of restoring the order of justice, it is nevertheless necessary to distinguish the various ways in which something can be contrary to one's will. Aquinas's understanding is broader than one might initially suspect, but, importantly, this breadth allows for greater flexibility in his conception of punishment. He argues that there are three different ways in which something can be contrary to one's will. It can be against man's actual will, his habitual will, or the very nature of the will itself.[37] The first is the most obvious and is not difficult to understand. The evil inflicted can be against the wrongdoer's actual will. In this case the punisher inflicts an evil or deprivation that the guilty person actively detests—imprisonment or a fine, for example. This is what usually comes to mind when we think of punishment and is punishment in the strictest sense.

The second form of punishment is when the evil is against the habitual will of the person. The example Aquinas gives here is when someone takes a piece of property without the owner's knowledge. The man habitually desires to remain in possession of his land, but *without his knowledge* it is taken away. Even though he does not know that this has happened, for Aquinas, it is still a real punishment because it contrasts with the man's habitual will. Were he to find out, it would then contrast with his actual will and would be an example of the first kind of punishment. Even more benign examples are conceivable, however. Imagine that a classroom of children habitually desires to play outside as much as possible. Nevertheless, they know that their class only has recess for thirty minutes a day. What they do not know is that their teacher was planning to give them extra recess on a given day. The children only habitually desire this extra recess, though, because they never *actually* considered it a possibility. When the teacher arrives, however, the children misbehave, and the teacher decides to revoke the planned but unannounced extra recess. Although the children do not know it, they have been punished. An evil (deprivation) has been imposed against their habitual will due to their misbehavior, and the equality of justice is restored to the classroom.

The third kind of punishment is when the evil merely contrasts with the natural inclination of the will. In this case what the wrongdoer receives

---

[37] *De malo,* q. 1, a. 4.

is in accordance with his actual will. He obtains what he desires actually, but it is against what his will desires by its own nature. Here Aquinas provides the example of a man who is deprived of a particular virtuous habit. The man by choice does not want to be virtuous, but he cannot change the fact that his will is naturally inclined to the good of virtue. Thus, in a real sense, his vice, though chosen, is against his will and is, therefore, a punishment.

The distinction between the first and the last two categories, between man's actual will and his habitual or natural will, also allows us to incorporate the notion of satisfaction into Aquinas's punitive theory. Satisfaction can be described as the voluntary acceptance of punishment for the sake of restoring justice.[38] It is a kind of freely chosen self-punishment. However, given what has been said about punishment, the very voluntary nature of satisfaction qualifies its punitive character. As Aquinas explains, "when punishment is satisfactory it loses somewhat of the nature of punishment: for the nature of punishment is to be against the will; and although satisfactory punishment, absolutely speaking, is against the will," either against one's habitual or natural will, "nevertheless in this particular case and for this particular purpose, it is voluntary"; that is, it is in accordance with one's actual will.[39] By a conditional but actual will, in other words, a man accepts something against his habitual or natural will for goods like health, money, or the free use of time, and so makes satisfaction to restore the equality of justice.

It should be noted, however, that this is only the core or most basic conception of satisfaction. Satisfaction, according to Aquinas, can never be anything less than the restoration of justice, but that does not mean that it cannot be *more* than that at the same time. In fact, by God's great mercy and providence, satisfaction in this life can also be both transformative[40] and meritorious.[41] In other words, satisfaction, because it is freely embraced, does not merely restore justice but also heals the person by strengthening his virtuous inclinations and deepens his friendship with God through an increase in the grace of charity. The voluntary character of satisfaction makes these additional advances possible. There is something of St. Paul's logic in this dynamic: "Where sin increased, grace abounded all the more."[42] The person who voluntarily makes satisfaction for past transgressions arrives by

---

[38] *Super Sent.*, lib. 4, dist. 15, q. 1, a. 1.

[39] *ST* Ia-IIae, q. 87, a. 6: "Poena autem satisfactoria diminuit aliquid de ratione poenae. Est enim de ratione poenae quod sit contra voluntatem. Poena autem satisfactoria, etsi secundum absolutam considerationem sit contra voluntatem, tamen tunc, et pro hoc, est voluntaria."

[40] *Super Sent.*, lib. 4, dist. 15, q. 1, a. 1, qc. 2, ad 2.

[41] *Super Sent.*, lib. 4, dist. 15, q. 1, a. 1, qc. 1, ad 1; a. 3, qc. 3.

[42] Rom 5:20.

the end of the process to a greater perfection than he possessed when he first sinned.[43] Nevertheless, despite this ascending movement, true satisfaction never abandons its basic orientation to the restoration of justice that is its defining characteristic.

Different Orders of Justice

To complete this cursory presentation of Aquinas's punitive theory it is also important to recognize the distinct orders of justice that distinguish different kinds of punishment. This returns us specifically to the question of the analogous use of the term "punishment," where our investigation began. In particular, the question is, how can we refer to both the immanent consequences of sin and the just punishment due to God from such acts as "temporal punishment" without reducing one to the other? The Orthodox and Protestants, as we saw, attempted to limit the divine punishment of the just to the immanent consequences of sin and did not recognize a distinct category of *reatus poenae*. Aquinas's account, however, acknowledges the harmony and relationship between the two without allowing such a reduction.

Aquinas rightly recognizes that man belongs to related but distinct orders of justice. Most basically, we are all subject to the order of reason. As social beings we are subject to a political community. Ultimately, however, we are all subject to God's providential government of the cosmos. Hence, just as there is a distinct justice in each of these orders, so too is there an appropriate and analogous punishment. Aquinas writes:

> Accordingly, man can be punished with a threefold punishment corresponding to the three orders to which the human will is subject. In the first place a man's nature is subjected to the order of his own reason; second, it is subjected to the order of another man who governs him either in spiritual or in temporal matters, as a member either of the state or of the household; third, it is subjected to the universal order of the Divine government. Now each of these orders is disturbed by sin, for the sinner acts against his reason, and against human and Divine law. Wherefore he incurs a threefold

---

[43] It would take us far afield and deserves a much more significant treatment than is possible here, but one can note that this notion of satisfaction plays an important part in Aquinas's understanding of the Passion. Because of Christ's exceeding charity and obedience his Passion possessed an infinite value. Thus, it cannot be reduced to the meager level of retributive justice as described by penal substitution theories. However, some aspect of just satisfaction is necessary to understand the Passion for Aquinas.

punishment; one, inflicted by himself, viz., remorse of conscience; another, inflicted by man; and a third, inflicted by God.[44]

This passage completes the body of the article that I quoted at the beginning of this section on Aquinas's punitive theory. Every order participates in some form of the natural inclination to repress the transgressor. However, distinct orders exercise that movement in different ways. Thus, as man is related to three distinct orders of justice, he is potentially subject to three different orders of punishment.

Although much can be said about the state and the necessity of civil punishment, this dimension does not fall within the bounds of our investigation. What is important for a proper understanding of purgatory is the relationship and distinction between, on the one hand, the punishments of the order of reason, and on the other, divine punishments properly speaking. In the section quoted above, Aquinas refers to "remorse of conscience" as the punishment for sin in the order of reason. Additionally, in the reply to the third objection he also notes that the "punishment of the *inordinate affection* is due to sin as overturning the order of reason."[45] Thus, there is a kind of twofold punishment even within the order of reason—one self-imposed (remorse) and one inherent in nature (an acquired inordinate affection). Both, however, correspond to the same order. From this we can see how Mark of Ephesus's emphasis on the subjective punishments of sin, such as remorse or contrition, still falls within the punishments from the order of reason, just as do the remaining personal moral imperfections that Kallistos Ware and the Protestants emphasized.

Following the previous affirmation, however, Aquinas then adds, "Nevertheless sin incurs a further punishment, through disturbing the order of the Divine or human law."[46] In other words, beyond the demand for punishment required to restore justice in the order of reason, there is a distinct necessity to restore equality to the order of divine justice or of

---

[44] *ST* Ia-IIae, q. 87, a. 1: "Unde secundum tres ordines quibus subditur humana voluntas, triplici poena potest homo puniri. Primo quidem enim subditur humana natura ordini propriae rationis; secundo, ordini exterioris hominis gubernantis vel spiritualiter vel temporaliter, politice seu oeconomice; tertio, subditur universali ordini divini regiminis. Quilibet autem horum ordinum per peccatum pervertitur, dum ille qui peccat, agit et contra rationem, et contra legem humanam, et contra legem divinam. Unde triplicem poenam incurrit, unam quidem a seipso, quae est conscientiae remorsus, aliam vero ab homine, tertiam vero a Deo."

[45] *ST* Ia-IIae, q. 87, a. 1, ad 3: "poena illa inordinati animi debetur peccato ex hoc quod ordinem rationis pervertit."

[46] *ST* Ia-IIae, q. 87, a. 1, ad 3: "Fit autem reus alterius poenae, per hoc quod pervertit ordinem legis divinae vel humanae."

human law. When it concerns the divine justice, this necessity (or obligation) is the irreducible *reatus poenae* in its strict sense which we have been discussing throughout this book. It cannot be identified with the inherent consequences of sin because the order of divine justice cannot be simply identified with the natural order of reason. There is a harmony, of course, between the two inasmuch as the natural law is man's participation in the eternal law.[47] Thus, we should not think of God's justice as somehow arbitrary or extrinsic to the created order. Our grasp of the natural law will certainly ground our understanding of the nature of divine justice, but the two are not thereby simply identical. Thus, just as the state is at times required to punish criminals to fully satisfy the demands of social justice, so too does divine justice often require more than the simple consequences of sin to restore order to God's creation. The two punishments, though both true punishments, are nevertheless distinct.

PUNISHMENT IN THE CHRISTIAN LIFE

It is the retributive value of punishment, particularly in light of divine justice, that thus allows us to fully grasp its place within God's providential care of man and lets the full picture emerge. In particular, if we keep in mind the distinction between the two orders of punishment, nature/reason and divine, a surprising beauty unfolds. As alluded to above, we will see the way that God in his wisdom masterfully interweaves the retributive, transformative, and meritorious dimensions of our purification.

Initially, at the beginning of the Christian life in baptism, man is justified and initiated into friendship with God. His divine life is just beginning. He is forgiven for all his past sins, and although he may have acquired a debt of punishment before divine justice, at the moment of his baptism the infinite satisfaction of Christ's Passion is applied to him perfectly "just as if he himself had offered sufficient satisfaction for all his sins."[48] He owes nothing more to divine justice. However, we cannot fail to notice that often the "temporal punishments" of the order of reason remain. This includes both those punishments due to original sin and those due to the actual sins he may have committed. The neophyte, excepting an extraordinary grace, for example, will consequently have to struggle against the same evil dispositions that he had acquired before baptism. Although he has been given new grace to fight against them, those remnants of sin still remain.

---

[47] *ST* Ia-IIae, q. 91, a. 2.

[48] *ST* IIIa, q. 69, a. 2: "ac si ipse sufficienter satisfecisset pro omnibus peccatis suis."

Nevertheless, we know that God does have the power to heal such things, even immediately. This is Aquinas's reading of the healing of Peter's mother-in-law in Luke 4:39—"immediately she rose and served them."[49] According to the angelic doctor, this physical healing is indicative of God's power to instantaneously heal the entire person. In like fashion, God could have taken away all of the punishments of sin for the newly baptized, but almost always he does not. If, though, there is no retributive value to those "punishments" of the order of reason (e.g., human weakness or residual evil dispositions)—the newly baptized has no *reatus poenae*—why does God allow them to remain?

The first reason that Aquinas gives is that they allow the Christian to be more conformed to Christ.[50] Jesus, too, though personally owing nothing to divine justice, willed to take on our sufferings—the temporal consequences of sin. As St. Peter reminds us, "He himself bore our sins in his body on the tree, that we might die to sin and live to righteousness."[51] He accepted the temporal punishments of sin so that he might make satisfaction for us. Similarly, the Christian, though just before God at the moment of baptism, is given the grace to accept the temporal consequences of sin in this world in order to share in Christ's satisfaction for others. St. Paul understood this well when he wrote to the Christians at Colossae, "Now I rejoice in my sufferings for your sake, and in my flesh I complete what is lacking in Christ's afflictions for the sake of his body, that is, the Church."[52] By baptism Christians are invited to join with Christ in making satisfaction for the sins of others.

Similarly, we saw above that satisfaction does not stop merely at rectifying the demands of justice but also leads to a meritorious increase in grace.[53] By God's gift and merciful dispensation, the soul who, prompted by the love of God, makes satisfaction for sin is thereby conformed more deeply to Christ. In other words, when man voluntarily participates in the satisfactory self-offering of Christ, God grants him a deeper share in the virtues of faith, hope, and charity in accordance with his promises. As St. Paul teaches, "each shall receive his wages according to his labor."[54] While it is beyond the scope of this book to examine the intricacies of the theology of merit, let it suffice to recognize a basic Catholic intuition about the performance of pious deeds and works of mercy. Although they have their own positive natural

---

[49] *ST* IIIa, q. 86, a. 5.

[50] *ST* IIIa, q. 69, a. 3.

[51] 1 Pet 2:24.

[52] Col 1:24.

[53] Cf. *Super Sent.*, lib. 4, dist. 15, q. 1, a. 1, qc. 1, ad 1; a. 3, qc. 3.

[54] 1 Cor 3:8.

consequence, God assists the souls who offer him this service of love with a greater holiness than the works alone are able to produce. For the context of this book, one must recognize that in a mysterious way it is a privilege and blessing to be able to suffer as Christ did.

This dimension also connects to Aquinas's second reason for why God allows the "punishments" of the order of reason, namely, our spiritual training.[55] The struggle, in other words, has a self-transformative value that redounds to the glory of God and man alike. By not simply healing our vices outright, God allows us to grow in discipline and perseverance. By patiently overcoming evil dispositions and the material imperfections of the fallen world we can win the "crown of victory."[56] The heroic and sublime perfection achieved by so many great saints testifies to this truth.

Finally, for the sake of completeness, Aquinas notes that the delayed healing of the temporal remnants of sin also ensures that people seek baptism only for the sake of its eternal value and not merely for temporal benefits.[57]

Thus, for these three reasons—the possibility of a meritorious increase in grace by voluntary conformity with Christ in his suffering, the spiritual training involved in the struggle against temptation, and the rejection of temporal motivations—God does not heal the soul at the moment of baptism or take away the struggles that lie ahead. Importantly, at this point the retributive aspect of punishment is not personally applicable. After baptism, so long as the person does not sin, just retribution only retains its value insofar as the Christian joins Christ in making satisfaction for the sins of the world. Instead, the transformative and meritorious dimensions of punishment are of primary importance.

The situation changes, however, when the Christian sins *after* baptism. Although the above reasons retain their validity, the retributive dimension now regains its personal dimension. This is because, as we will see in more detail in chapter five, the sacrament of penance does not always remit the entire debt of punishment before divine justice like baptism does. Christ has certainly still made perfect satisfaction in his Passion, but in the sacrament of penance, according to Aquinas, "man shares in the power of Christ's Passion *according to the measure of his own acts. . . .* Wherefore the entire debt of punishment is not remitted at once after the first act of penance, by which act the guilt is remitted, but only when all the acts of penance have been

---

55 *ST* IIIa, q. 69, a. 3.

56 *ST* IIIa, q. 69, a. 3: "victoriae coronam."

57 *ST* IIIa, q. 69, a. 3.

completed."[58] In other words, postbaptismal forgiveness of sins requires man's cooperation in his own satisfaction. This is the very logic of the penance imposed by the priest. The contrite and forgiven sinner cooperates with the grace of Christ, bearing worthy fruits of repentance, and thereby shares in the satisfaction Christ has won for him. Thus, the process of purification for these postbaptismal sins is then simultaneously retributive, transformative, and meritorious during this life.

From this perspective of the plenary renewal of the sinner in the sacramental life of grace, we can see better the harmony even in the midst of distinction between the two orders of justice as Aquinas would have us understand them. Though the two orders do not become identical to one another, because of their hierarchical relationship one punishment can satisfy justice at multiple levels if appropriately integrated. Just as Christ, for example, could voluntarily accept the temporal punishments of original sin in human nature as a worthy means to make satisfaction before God for all of man's sins, so too can our loving acceptance of suffering (regularly due to our own failings) help to make satisfaction before divine justice.[59] Often, however, such a spiritual disposition, though both valuable and foundational, does not fully suffice to establish equality before divine justice, and additional practices of self-denial and penance are necessary. It is thus not only in accepting the sufferings of this life but in actively denying ourselves that we make perfect satisfaction.

CONCLUSION

The distinction in unity between the orders of justice outlined in this final section accords with the truth we saw at the beginning of this chapter in the biblical examples. The history of God's people continually saw the harmonious integration of the retributive, transformative, and meritorious dimensions of the divine decree of punishment. In what was the most illuminative example, we saw how David was progressively forgiven, punished, and transformed. Such a vision allows us to both recognize and deepen the insight of Barnard that was discussed in the previous chapter. As we saw, he identified the good of the process of moral transformation as the reason why God does not instantly perfect those who come to saving faith. Our analysis

---

[58] *ST* IIIa, q. 86, a. 4, ad 3 (emphasis mine): "[C]onsequitur virtutem passionis Christi secundum modum propriorum actuum. . . . Et ideo non statim per primum actum poenitentiae, quo remittitur culpa, solvitur reatus totius poenae, sed completis omnibus poenitentiae actibus."

[59] CCC, §1473.

in this chapter confirms his understanding but specifies the nature of this good in a way that Barnard was unable to. The process is good because it is retributive, transformative, and meritorious. Without these motivations God would have no reason not to bring the just to immediate moral perfection.

Nevertheless, as I noted before, Barnard recognizes death as an arbitrary point in the process of transformation. He sees no reason why God's action toward the soul would change at that moment. If the process is good, let the process continue. However, the Catholic understanding of death and the particular judgment does not allow us to see death as a merely arbitrary point. As I have already noted, at the particular judgment the soul's eternal fate is decreed and the possibility of merit or demerit is ended. The soul remains with as much charity as it possessed at the moment of death. Thus, there is a significant change, and death is not an arbitrary moment. The meritorious aspect of the process of transformation is no longer applicable. The souls in purgatory do not grow in charity by undergoing purification. Thus, only the retributive and transformative dimensions remain.

However, even though this transformative aspect may still be relevant (a point we can presume for now but which must be argued in the next chapter against the position of Bellarmine and others like him), further analysis shows that the retributive aspect takes priority after a person's death. Along with the Catholic tradition, Aquinas affirms that those who are baptized and who have acquired no debt of punishment before divine justice for personal sins committed after baptism go immediately to heaven.[60] This is the teaching confirmed by the Council of Florence[61] and referred to in the *Catechism of the Catholic Church*.[62] At baptism, the soul is completely justified, and, although certain remnants of sin (punishments of sin according to the order of reason) do remain, they do not independently justify a delay of union with God after death. Certainly, they need to be purified before one can fully enter into the bliss of heaven, but, as we saw in Aquinas's interpretation of the cure of Peter's mother-in-law, in unique circumstances God can and does heal them immediately. If he does not, as the doctrine of purgatory as I have presented it here suggests, it is because there remains a retributive value to the soul's submission to the process of transformation. The equality before divine justice is still lacking, and God,

---

[60] *Super Sent.*, lib. 4, dist. 2, q. 2, a. 1, qc. 3, ad 4.

[61] Denzinger, §1316. "Huius sacramenti effectus est remissio omnis culpae originalis et actualis, omnis quoque poenae, quae pro ipsa culpa debetur. Propterea baptizatis nulla pro peccatis praeteritis iniungenda est satisfactio: sed morientes, antequam culpam aliquam committant, statim ad regnum caelorum et Dei visionem perveniunt."

[62] CCC, §1263.

therefore, allows the punitive transformation of the sinner to continue.[63] In other words, since the meritorious value of progressive transformation is no longer present in purgatory, it is only the retributive value of said process that justifies its protraction. When God has neither reasons of retribution nor of merit to slowly bring about the transformation of man, he heals him immediately. Thus, contra the Orthodox and Protestants whom we have seen in this book, even if we maintain and incorporate the transformative dimension of purification, purgatory can only be understood by reference to the unique demands of divine justice for proper satisfaction.

---

[63] Nevertheless, this punishment takes place in a unique way in accordance with the state of the soul at that time, as we will see.

CHAPTER IV

The Two Theories of Purgatory

IN THE LAST CHAPTER I argued, in light of Aquinas's punitive theory, that purgatory must be understood as a punitive process with a retributive value. The only sufficient reason that a soul possessed of charity at the moment of death does not immediately enter into the joy of eternal beatitude is because it still has some debt before divine justice.[1] This can either be from remaining unforgiven venial sins or from sins already forgiven but still only imperfectly satisfied for. This is the central claim of the Catholic doctrine of purgatory.

---

[1]   Note that this is the only *sufficient* reason. As I will argue, the moral transformation of the soul is also a reason for purgatory, but it is subordinate in purgatory to the retributive motive and by itself would be insufficient to justify the delay of full beatitude entailed by purgatory. Certainly CCC, §1472 does state that "every sin, even venial, entails an unhealthy attachment to creatures, which must be purified either here on earth, or after death in the state called Purgatory." I argue, however, that this passage from the Catechism presents the typical pattern of human purgation after death in which the need for retribution and transformation are intertwined. In this case the unhealthy attachment to creatures must be purified in purgatory if not completed on earth. Nevertheless, as I will explain in more detail in this chapter, in the event that the person is completely justified before God in the order of divine justice (with no need for retributive punishment) then the unhealthy attachments that remain after death would primarily be purified at the first moment of encounter with God after death and perfected upon entrance into the beatific vision. The Catechism passage presented here does not touch on this aspect of the doctrine, but I believe the argument I propose is linked with other firmly held doctrines of the faith in such a way that we are required to read that particular passage of the Catechism in the manner I have described. In particular, I argue that it is the only way to reconcile CCC, §1472 with CCC, §1263, which states, "By Baptism all sins are forgiven, original sin and all personal sins, as well as all punishment for sin. In those who have been reborn nothing remains that would impede their entry into the Kingdom of God, neither Adam's sin, nor personal sin, nor the consequences of sin, the gravest of which is separation from God." If nothing remains that would impede their entry into the Kingdom of God, then the unhealthy attachments to creatures which clearly do remain after baptism must not be sufficient to impede entrance into heaven, at least not by themselves.

Aquinas, for instance, regularly grounds his explanation and defense of purgatory in an understanding of the *reatus poenae*. In his commentary on the *Sentences* he writes, "For if after guilt is effaced through contrition, the debt of punishment is not entirely taken away. . . . God's justice requires that . . . a person who dies after contrition and absolution for sin but before making the due satisfaction must be punished after this life."[2] Similarly, in the *Compendium theologiae* he writes, "Since the order of divine justice demands that punishment be undergone for sins, we must hold that souls pay after this life the penalty they have not paid while on earth."[3] We find a like wording in many of the conciliar and magisterial proclamations of the Church about purgatory as well.[4]

Presumably, the debates with the Orthodox and Protestants over this matter during the last millennium led to a solidification of this understanding in the minds of Catholic theologians. It became a matter of primary importance to defend purgatory on precisely this point. Thus, as I mentioned in chapter two, Bellarmine and Suarez focus nearly all of their attention on the debt of justice. It is the quasi-exclusive object of purification after this life for them. Although there was no lack of theological reasoning for this concentration (some of which we have already seen and will return to shortly), as a matter of historical conjecture, it seems possible that the apologetic importance of arguments about satisfaction and justice may also have contributed in part to such an exclusive emphasis on this dimension.

Nevertheless, even though retributive satisfaction is the primary theological reason for purgatory, this does not necessarily mean that it is the only one. St. John Paul II, for instance, highlighted the medicinal and transformative dimension of man's eschatological purification in one of his general audiences.[5] We also saw briefly in chapter two that Garrigou-Lagrange argued similarly. In short, they both taught that the punishments of purgatory had a transformative value. The evil dispositions of the soul, in other

---

2   *Super Sent.*, lib. 4, dist. 21, q. 1, a. 1, qc. 1: "Si enim per contritionem deleta culpa non tollitur ex toto reatus poenae . . . justitia Dei hoc exigit ut . . . ille qui post contritionem de peccato et absolutionem decedit ante satisfactionem debitam, quod post hanc vitam puniatur."

3   *Compendium theologiae*, lib. 1, cap. 181: "Et quia ordo divinae iustitiae habet ut pro culpis poenae reddantur, oportet dicere, quod post hanc vitam animae poenam exsolvunt quam in hoc mundo non exsolverunt."

4   Denzinger, *Compendium*, §§856, 1066, 1304, 1398, 1580; Paul VI, *Indulgentiarum Doctrina*, §§3, 4.

5   John Paul II, General Audience of September 29, 1999, accessed March 9, 2020, http://www.vatican.va/content/john-paul-ii/en/audiences/1999/documents/hf_jp-ii_aud_29091999.html.

words, are healed progressively through the righteous soul's experience of a just punishment.

However, besides a few similar examples, there is hardly sufficient evidence in the magisterium or in the Church's tradition to make the case for a consistent or unanimous teaching that purgatorial punishments are necessarily medicinal. As we also saw, Jugie, a leading theologian on purgatory in the first half of the twentieth century, disagreed with Garrigou-Lagrange on this particular reading of Aquinas. He, along with Bellarmine and Suarez, did not attribute any medicinal effect to divine punishment in purgatory. For one reason or another, as we will see in more detail below, the soul is not personally healed through the experience of suffering. Purgatory, for these theologians, is merely an exercise of divine justice aimed at obtaining the required retributive punishment. To put it succinctly, the difference between these two schools of thought lies with the question of whether moral transformation happens at some particular instant after death (and therefore does not directly accompany punishment) or whether it comes about progressively *through* the soul's experience of punishment. Because of this debate, in the era of Jugie and Garrigou-Lagrange it became common to refer to the two theories of purgatory.[6]

In this chapter I will attempt to defend the Thomistic position advocated by Garrigou-Lagrange and John Paul II against that of Bellarmine and those like him. Having said that, however, one important clarification is in order. Contra both Garrigou-Lagrange and Jugie, I do not believe that Aquinas himself gives us a definitive position on this question in his writings. According to my reading, he only explicitly addresses it in one place in an early text.[7] However, even there the purification of the powers (and their habits) is only tangential to his principal argument, and his understanding of the main thesis of that text has changed in such a way in his mature thought that his position there on the rectification of the evil dispositions should not be taken as representative of his definitive position. This passage deserves some analysis, but we do better to wait until the end of the chapter when we will have a fuller sense of the nature of the question and when the relevant aspects of Aquinas's mature position will have been presented.

For now, it is best to presume that Aquinas did not articulate a definitive position on the question. The history and existence of the debate suggests

---

[6]   Cf. Mother Mary of St. Austin, *The Divine Crucible of Purgatory*, rev. and ed. Nicholas Ryan, S.J. (Newport News, VA: Providence Foundation, 1940), 15–19. The passage cited was added posthumously by the editor.

[7]   *Super Sent.*, lib. 4, dist. 21, q. 1, a. 3, qc. 1.

as much. Even the passage that Garrigou-Lagrange presents in favor of his view admits of being read in a different way. As we saw, Aquinas writes, "the harshness of the penalty properly corresponds to the quantity of fault, but the duration corresponds to how rooted the fault was in the subject."[8] According to Garrigou-Lagrange, Aquinas is here clearly suggesting that the uprooting of the residual evil dispositions is in some way an intrinsic determining factor of the length of punishment, in the sense that the punishment is done when the uprooting is complete. However, Aquinas can also just as easily be read as simply expressing the *ratio* of the measurement of divine justice from God's perspective. In other words, lest God's decree be completely arbitrary, there must be some metric to account for the "amount" of punishment owed in terms of duration, and here Aquinas is giving us his description of that scale. Of all of Aquinas's passages about purgatory this is the most suggestive of a transformative reading, but it is obscure at best. It is safer to conclude, therefore, that he simply does not have a definitive position that we can easily turn to in any of his writings.

Nevertheless, the question of the rectification of evil dispositions is not foreign to the system proposed by Aquinas. As I showed in chapter one, a Thomistic anthropology both permits and invites us to consider it, and subsequent theological debates make this inquiry all the more important. Using Aquinas's principles and without contradicting any of his definitive teachings on purgatory, I believe that a transformative account of purgatorial punishments can still be both proposed and defended. Certainly, because of the complexity and ambiguity of the question and its history, this chapter will be the most original and, therefore, also the most provisional of the book. It will suffer from the limitations inherent in any attempt to use Aquinas to answer a question that he himself appears not to have directly asked. However, I believe it can be argued that the transformative dimension of purgatory actually provides the interior and subjective ground for a just and fitting punishment—one that accords best with God's surpassing justice, goodness, and wisdom. The most fitting punishment, in other words, is the one that transforms us.

STATE OF THE SEPARATED SOUL

Before considering the precise nature of purgatorial punishments, however, it is necessary to first describe the state of the soul separated from the body

---

[8] *Super sent.,* lib. 4, dist. 21, q. 1, a. 3, qc. 3, ad 1: "acerbitas poenae proprie respondet quantitati culpae; sed diuturnitas respondet radicationi culpae in subjecto."

at death. Some of what was presumed at the beginning of the first chapter, particularly regarding the permanent orientation of the moral character of the soul after death, will now have to be examined in more detail. The unique state of the soul after death and separation from the body affects in significant ways how it might be punished or transformed.

First it must be reiterated that the soul is the form of the body. Thus, its natural condition is incarnate. The body is not a prison for the soul but its home. Without being limited to sensible reality, the intellectual soul was, nevertheless, created by God to operate within the material world. Under these normal conditions, the soul "can only understand by turning to the phantasms,"[9] that is, the material sense images produced by the brain. Although the soul's proper intellectual operation and knowledge are intrinsically independent of matter (it is not a material process like digestion, for example), the mind nevertheless depends on the body to operate normally.

This ordinary mode of operation, however, is no longer possible after separation from the body. The sense faculties, unlike the intellectual faculties, are intrinsically connected to the body and have no proper action apart from the material organs which operate. In fact, the subject of the sense faculties is the body-soul composite, so, in a proper sense, the sense faculties cease to exist in act after the death of the body.[10] Deprived of these faculties, the mind has no sense images to turn to, since all sensory activity (up to and including imagination) is impeded in this state.[11] All that remains in the soul are the superior faculties of intellect and will, the dispositions of those powers, and the knowledge contained therein.[12]

Under these unique circumstances, the soul begins to operate in a

---

[9] *ST* Ia, q. 88, a. 1: "nihil intelligit nisi convertendo se ad phantasmata."

[10] Admittedly, the sense faculties do continue to exist in the separated soul as in their root and principle (see *Super Sent.*, lib. 4, dist. 44, q. 3, a. 3, qc. 1; Réginald Garrigou-Lagrange, *Reality*, trans. Patrick Cummins, O.S.B. [St. Louis: B. Herder Books, 1950], 193), but this affirmation seeks to affirm the integrity of the separated soul rather than the continued existence of the sense powers in any real, active sense. Because the powers exist in this seminal way in the separated soul, they will not have to be recreated at the resurrection of the body, but to admit this point is not to say that they continue to exist in act in the separated soul. It should similarly be noted that the habits of the sense faculties also cease to exist after the death of the body. That being said, there may still be significant residual evil dispositions in need of purification in the separated soul. The intellect and will, after all, are responsible for every act of sin, and the habits of these spiritual powers do remain. Thus, if any evil dispositions continue to characterize these powers they will need to be rectified before the soul can enter into heaven. We have seen this nuance before and will see it again toward the end of this chapter. See also *De anima*, q. 19.

[11] Garrigou-Lagrange, *Life Everlasting*, 87–88.

[12] Garrigou-Lagrange, *Life Everlasting*, 88.

quasi-angelic manner. Rather than understanding things through material sense images, now "[the soul] has a mode of understanding, by turning to simply intelligible objects, as is proper to other separate substances," that is, the angels.[13] They receive these intelligible species "from the influence of the Divine light."[14] Such a cognitive mode, however, though nobler than man's typical sense-imbedded thinking, is difficult for us since we have such a weak intellect. If this was the only kind of understanding available to man, our knowledge would be only confused and general.[15] We simply do not have the ability to draw out the hidden riches of such pure and sublime ideas as do the angels. We remain overwhelmed and almost blinded by the brightness of the things above us. It is more natural and comfortable for man to gain knowledge from the material world one piece at a time.

In accordance with this state, the separated soul is infallibly fixed in its moral orientation at death. According to Aquinas, during this life the basic disposition of the soul is "accidentally subject to change in accordance with some change in the body."[16] He has in mind here the sensitive faculties in particular, with both the passions and the information derived from sensation. These constantly propose different objects to the mind or present new information about already known objects. Insofar as each of these is good, it competes for the desire of the will. Consequently, man is capable of making any good his final end, from the noblest to the basest. By charity, however, he orders these created goods to the true ultimate good—God himself. A lack of charity, as we have seen, is when man chooses any other good as his final end.

After death, however, this disposition remains fixed. There is no new information or perspective that can alter the soul's decision. Instead the soul can only continue in line with the prior disposition of its will. Aquinas explains, "when [the soul] departs from the body, it will no longer be in a state of mobility toward the end, but of resting in the end. Consequently, the will, as regards the desire for the ultimate end, will be immovable."[17] In the separated state it sees the basic reality of good and evil so clearly and

---

[13] *ST* Ia, q. 89, a. 1: "competit ei modus intelligendi per conversionem ad ea quae sunt intelligibilia simpliciter, sicut et aliis substantiis separatis."

[14] *ST* Ia, q. 89, a. 3: "ex influentia divini luminis."

[15] *ST* Ia, q. 89, a. 1.

[16] *SCG* IV, cap. 95: "Dispositio enim animae movetur per accidens secundum aliquem motum corporis."

[17] *SCG* IV, cap. 95: "Quando igitur erit a corpore separata, non erit in statu ut moveatur ad finem, sed ut in fine adepto quiescat. Immobilis igitur erit voluntas eius quantum ad desiderium ultimi finis."

instantaneously that nothing can make it change its choice.[18] The separated souls become, in that regard, like the angels. Those with charity, whether in heaven or in purgatory, will rejoice in the good; those without charity will detest it.

This affirmation accounts for the impeccability of the souls in purgatory with regard to mortal sin, but it should be added that their sinlessness also extends to venial sins.[19] This idea, however, easily follows from what I said above. Venial sin, as we saw, is not a change in ultimate disposition (now no longer possible) but merely a deviation in the ordering of means to that end. Such a deviation is caused by a slight turning to the creature. In the separated state, however, this small lapse is no longer possible. For one, the sense passions (in particular the *fomes*)[20] no longer affect the soul and therefore cease drawing the soul constantly to every passing good. Similarly, the perception of truth in the pure intelligible species is too immediate to allow for misunderstanding or distraction. The simplified life of these souls together with their charity leaves only one thing on their minds—to do the will of God.

Time for the Separated Soul

Nevertheless, although the will is fixed immovably in the good, along with the intellect it does experience change as it moves from object to object. Aquinas explains, "the will of the separated soul is not changeable from good to evil, although it is changeable from the desire for one thing to the desire for another, provided the order to the ultimate end be observed."[21] In other words, although the end does not change, the various means to that end do change at any given time. This truth follows from the fact that the soul cannot possibly consider all things at once. It must pass from one object to the next. As Aquinas indicates, the soul's desires accompany this movement, reacting with appropriate love or hatred to the good or evil that comes before it.

Consequently, there is a kind of experience of succession and change for the separated soul. Such, of course, is presumed by the doctrine of purgatory, which describes the *process* of the soul's purification. Any process necessarily involves a movement from one state to another. To put it simply, it involves

---

[18] Garrigou-Lagrange, *Life Everlasting*, 65–66.

[19] *Super Sent.*, lib. 4, dist. 21, q. 1, a. 3, qc. 1, ad 2.

[20] *Super Sent.*, lib. 4, dist. 21, q. 1, a. 3, qc. 1, ad 2.

[21] *SCG* IV, cap. 95. "Non est igitur voluntas animae separatae mutabilis de bono in malum: licet sit mutabilis de uno volito in aliud, servato tamen ordine ad eundem ultimum finem."

change. Time, therefore, as the measurement of change, also has its place in purgatory.

That being said, the kind of time which describes change in purgatory is quite different from earthly time, in accordance with the unique state of the separated soul. The separated soul's movement from object to object is discontinuous. These spiritual "moments" do not flow seamlessly one into the next as do moments on earth. On earth, we might say, the movement or change is continuous. It is marked most frequently by the daily, unceasing rotation of the earth. For the separated soul, in contrast, the movement is punctiliar. Garrigou-Lagrange thus refers to time in purgatory as "discontinuous time."[22] He writes, "Discontinuous time, then, is opposed to continuous or solar time. It is found in angels and separated souls, as the measure of successive thoughts and affections. One thought lasts for one spiritual instant."[23] He illustrates the idea by describing the ecstasy of a great saint. The saint, so he explains, can be rapt in a single thought for a period of two or more hours.[24] In a similar way, the souls in purgatory pass from one spiritual thought and affection to the next and so undergo their purification in discontinuous time.[25] In our examination of purgatory, then, we must analyze the successive, discontinuous moments that mark their purification. This approach will become clearer in its application.[26]

---

[22] Garrigou-Lagrange, *Life Everlasting*, 90.

[23] Garrigou-Lagrange, *Life Everlasting*, 90–91.

[24] Garrigou-Lagrange, *Life Everlasting*, 91.

[25] I intentionally make no mention here of the traditional allocation of days to particular indulgences. I will discuss the meaning of that metric in chapter six.

[26] For the sake of completeness, it is fitting to mention that, according to Aquinas, in a broader sense, the time of the separated soul as well as that of the angels is properly called "aeviternity" (*ST* Ia, q. 10, a. 5.). It is a kind of mean between eternity and time. Eternity, according to the Boethian definition that Aquinas adopts, is "the simultaneously-whole and perfect possession of interminable life" (*ST* Ia, q. 10, a. 1). To put it simply, it is the measure of God's changelessness. Time, in contrast, is the measure of creaturely change (*ST* Ia, q. 10, a. 4). Aeviternity, however, as the mean between the two, measures those creatures whose being "neither consists in change, nor is the subject of change . . . [but who nevertheless] have change annexed to them either actually or potentially" (*ST* Ia, q. 10, a. 4). It is the measure, in other words, proper to angels and human souls on account of their substantial immutability and incorruptibility. Garrigou-Lagrange's presentation, which I have been following above, by distinguishing discontinuous time simply accentuates the distinction already present in Aquinas's understanding between substantial immutability and accidental change.

For Garrigou-Lagrange, it is better to consider the "time" of the separated soul as subject to a "double kind of duration"—aeviternity, which describes their substantial changelessness and discontinuous time which measures the succession of ideas (Garrigou-Lagrange, *Life Everlasting*, 90–91). He writes, "Eviternity measures what is immutable in angels and separated souls. It is

THE PARTICULAR JUDGMENT

The first of these spiritual moments for the separated soul is its particular judgment. In this instant God judges the charity of the soul and declares its eternal fate. The examination of the case and pronouncement of the sentence are both instantaneous.[27] As Garrigou-Lagrange explains:

> At the moment of separation the soul knows itself without medium. It is enlightened, decisively and inevitably, on all its merits and demerits. It sees its state without possibility of error, sees all that it has thought, desired, said, and done, both in good and in evil. It sees all the good it has omitted. Memory and conscience penetrate its entire moral and spiritual life, even to the minutest details.[28]

Such an experience follows from the unique state of the separated soul as I presented it above. There is a new, natural, intuitive awareness of one's own life and being. This personal insight is matched by God's divine judgment of the soul. He knows our every thought and deed and shows us their true worth. "Intellectual illumination awakes all acquired ideas, gives additional infused ideas, whereby the soul sees its entire past in a glance. The soul sees how God judges, and conscience makes this judgment definitive."[29] Though he can detest it, man can no longer deny the truth that God declares.

The fitting reward or punishment of the soul then follows immediately, though in a second moment.[30] The damned, as the Church has always understood, descend straight to hell and begin to experience their eternal punishment. With respect to the righteous, however, the situation is more complex, and it is at this precise moment that the position of Garrigou-Lagrange begins to depart from that of Bellarmine and Suarez. Among the holy souls, though all possess charity, many still retain some combination of unforgiven venial sins, residual evil dispositions, and a debt of

---

the measure of their substance, of their natural knowledge of self and God. Eviternity excludes succession" (Garrigou-Lagrange, *Life Everlasting*, 90–91). He continues, "[Discontinuous time] is found in angels and separated souls, as the measure of successive thoughts and affections" (Garrigou-Lagrange, *Life Everlasting*, 91). For our purposes the distinction is a helpful one since the study of purgatory focuses precisely on those aspects of the separated soul which undergo change. Garrigou-Lagrange's description of discontinuous time helps by clarifying more precisely the nature of that succession.

27 Garrigou-Lagrange, *Life Everlasting*, 73–74.

28 Garrigou-Lagrange, *Life Everlasting*, 73–74.

29 Garrigou-Lagrange, *Life Everlasting*, 74.

30 Cf. Garrigou-Lagrange, *Life Everlasting*, 75. "At the moment of the particular judgment the soul does not see God intuitively, otherwise it would already be beatified."

punishment before divine justice. As I have argued, these must be addressed first. However, as the last chapter showed, the residual evil dispositions alone are not sufficient to merit a delay in the reward. How, then, are they rectified?

Since the need for this transformation of the habits is sometimes common both to those who go immediately to heaven and to those who spend time in purgatory, one plausible theological explanation is to posit a unique mode of rectification, one that could simultaneously account for this change in both groups. Such a mode would necessarily correspond to the experience undergone by the soul at a given moment, and so, for proponents of this theory, there are two possible moments to examine: the particular judgment and the first instant of beatification. These are the two moments shared by both groups. For the souls who go immediately to heaven, the second moment immediately follows the first. For the souls in need of purgatory, the first comes before their punishments and the second comes after. If there is only one mode of transformation, it must correspond to one of these two moments.

To be fair, the idea that the particular judgment rectifies all residual dispositions is not so difficult to imagine. The divine illumination of that moment, by virtue of the soul's charity, is accompanied by generous, loving acceptance. The soul assents to God's penetrating judgment, recognizing both faults and merits nearly imperceptible to ordinary observation. According to many authors, this movement of charity is so complete and powerful that by it all unforgiven venial sins are remitted with respect to guilt.[31] Aquinas cites this argument in an objection of question seven, article eleven of *De malo*. He writes, "A great evil, namely, the bitter pain of purgatory, threatens the separated soul liable to the punishment of purgatory, and the separated soul is kept from the good most hoped for, namely, eternal life. Therefore an intense desire immediately arises in the separated soul. But intensity of charity is incompatible with venial sin."[32] The objection then concludes that therefore no venial sin would be remitted in purgatory. Aquinas, however, responds, "The argument of this objection validly concludes that venial sin is instantly remitted in purgatory, not that venial sin is not remitted there. And this seems quite likely."[33] The act of love and the

---

[31] Garrigou-Lagrange, *Life Everlasting*, 180–81.

[32] *De malo*, q. 7, a. 11, obj. 16: "Sed animae separatae quae est Purgatorio obnoxia, imminet magnum malum, scilicet acerba Purgatorii poena, et differtur a maximo bono separato, scilicet a vita aeterna. Ergo statim excitatur in ea fervens desiderium. Sed fervor caritatis non compatitur secum veniale."

[33] *De malo*, q. 7, a. 11, ad 16: "Ad decimumsextum dicendum, quod illa ratio non concludit quod peccatum veniale in Purgatorio non remittatur, sed quod statim ibi remittatur; et hoc satis videtur probabile."

repentance virtually included in it powerfully bring about the forgiveness of all remaining venial sins.

It is conceivable, then, that the total rectification of the soul also accompanies this powerful act of love. Such, in fact, is precisely the argument of Bellarmine. As we saw, he writes:

> It is believable that all these habits are abolished by the first contrary act of the separated soul, which it elicits immediately from separation. For, even if this habit, contracted in one act, cannot be destroyed by many acts, nevertheless, there it will be able to be [destroyed by that first contrary act] because the act will be much more forceful, seeing that then the soul will be more powerful in regard to spiritual acts and it will not have the contrary *fomites* and resistance as it has here.[34]

His argument has a certain plausibility. The "conversion" of that moment, if we can call it that, will be more powerful than anything many of us have ever experienced here on earth. However, *mutatis mutandis*, ordinary experience often shows that even deep, genuine contrition is not always accompanied by perfect moral rectification. The perception and acceptance of the truth is not the same as the interior perfection of all moral habits. Such is the reality of the human struggle with sin. It seems fair to recognize that the moral transformation *begins* in that moment, but it is not obvious that it is *completed* in that moment. As in this life, it is likely that the soul in that state still needs time to conform to the truth already perceived and accepted.

A different argument from Aquinas also challenges those who seek to identify the particular judgment as the unique moment of moral transformation after death. In the *Summa contra Gentiles* Aquinas describes the perfection of the wills of the blessed in their possession of the beatific vision.[35] He writes:

> The good, as such, is lovable. Therefore, that which is apprehended as supremely good is most lovable. Now in seeing God, the beatified rational substance apprehends him as supremely good; therefore, it loves God above all things. Moreover, it is a part of love that those who love each other should be of one will. Therefore, the will of the blessed is perfectly conformed to God, since the divine will is

---

[34] Bellarmine, *On Purgatory*, 198.
[35] *SCG* IV, cap. 92.

the supreme rule of all wills: and consequently the will of those who see God cannot be perverse.[36]

Because God is Goodness itself, the vision and perfect possession of him in the beatific vision overwhelms and floods all of the soul's desires. Standing face-to-face with Goodness himself, the will could not persist in its residual imperfections. It is conformed perfectly to the will of God in every way.

It is important to recognize the profound difference between this vision and the spiritual insight of the soul at the moment of the particular judgment. At the particular judgment the soul understands perfectly its own moral state—the truth about itself and about God. However, there still remains a certain obscurity and distance. The end is not yet fully obtained. In the beatific vision, however, not simply the truth about oneself and about God but Truth and Goodness himself is possessed by the soul. Great though the particular judgment will be, it is infinitely less than this first moment of heavenly beatitude.

If, therefore, Aquinas means that the beatific vision causes the requisite perfection of the soul,[37] then proponents of a unique mode and moment of rectification should consider instead the first instant of beatitude. This, as I said, is the second moment that both those who pass directly to heaven and those who spend time in purgatory share in common. If their rectification is not accomplished at the particular judgment it could reasonably take place in the first moment of heaven. Such, in fact, was a possibility considered by

---

[36] *SCG* IV, cap. 92: "Bonum, inquantum huiusmodi, diligibile est. Quod igitur apprehenditur ut optimum, est maxime diligibile. Sed substantia rationalis beata videns Deum, apprehendit ipsum ut optimum. Ergo maxime ipsum diligit. Hoc autem habet ratio amoris, quod voluntates se amantium sint conformes. Voluntates igitur beatorum sunt maxime conformes Deo: quod facit rectitudinem voluntatis, cum divina voluntas sit prima regula omnium voluntatum. Voluntates igitur Deum videntium non possunt fieri perversae."

[37] To be fair, this passage from Aquinas does not unambiguously argue that the vision itself is perfective of the will. His account of the will of the blessed—"is perfectly conformed to God"—could be read either descriptively or causatively. In other words, one could take him to mean that this perfect conformity is an *effect* of the beatific vision, or one could take him to mean that this perfect conformity is a *prerequisite* for the beatific vision. Grammatically, the English "is conformed" can be read as a passive verb, but the original Latin adjectival form "*sunt conformes*" is not a passive construction and has no inherent connotation of an action received. This initially lends credence to the descriptive reading. Nevertheless, the Latin does include a line that did not make it into the English translation: "Voluntates igitur beatorum sunt maxime conformes Deo: *quod facit rectitudinem voluntatis*, cum divina voluntas sit prima regula omnium voluntatum." The key line is italicized—"this produces rectitude of will." This clause, then, suggests the causative reading in which it is the vision of God itself which fully perfects the will.

Suarez. He writes, as we saw, that "all the natural virtues [might be] infused *per accidens* by reason of the status of the soul on its first entry into glory, and these [would] expel the repugnant habits."[38] The gift of the beatitude, according to this account, would overflow throughout the soul, rendering every faculty perfect and wiping out every residual defect.

Again, such a theory is plausible and has substantial support in sound theological reasoning. The first moment of the beatific vision very well may have a profound perfective effect in the soul[39] and, since it is shared, can equally account for this change in both those who go immediately to heaven and those who pass through purgatory.

Nevertheless, a certain difficulty arises here for proponents of a unique moment of rectification at the entrance into beatitude. This claim would commit its adherents to the corollary that the experience of the particular judgment is *not* rectifying. In this theory, all transformation must wait until the end, lest we begin to multiply modalities. If held exclusively, there is, then, an opposition between the theories of Bellarmine and Suarez presented here. If they or their disciples insist on a single mode of rectification, in other words, the two options are mutually exclusive.

In light of such a difficulty, it seems much more reasonable to posit not one but two modes of rectification for the separated soul, one which begins the transformation and one which perfects it. This theory has many advantages. First, it allows us to preserve the insights of both of these great theologians. Bellarmine and Suarez both present convincing and yet imperfect accounts of the soul's transformation. When combined, a fuller picture emerges.[40] At the moment of the particular judgment the soul's profound act of love begins to iron out the residual evil dispositions that remain latent in the soul. It may happen, however, that more remains than can be removed by a single act, strong though it may be. Only later, upon the soul's entrance into heaven, is the soul crowned with the ultimate perfection, which even an infinite series of acts could not grant it.

More importantly, however, the other advantage of this theory is that it acknowledges the possible need for continued transformation after the

---

[38] Francisco Suarez, "De Purgatorio," disp. 47, §1, no. 5: "aut certe in primo ingressu gloriae ratione status infunduntur per accidens omnes virtutes etiam naturales, quae habitus repugnantes expellunt" (translation mine).

[39] Cf. Garrigou Lagrange, *Life Everlasting*, 188–89.

[40] To be fair, immediate rectification at beatification is only one possibility considered by Suarez. He does list other potential means of healing of the habits. However, he gives no account of how they might be integrated or coordinated and does not seem to view them as an integral part of the purgation process as I am attempting to present it.

particular judgment, as did Suarez, while recognizing a mode of transformation that does not require the beatific vision, as did Bellarmine. When combined in this way, the unified vision enables us to consider the possibility of ongoing transformation in purgatory. It is conceivable, in other words, that the mode of transformation begun in the particular judgment continues with the punishments of purgatory and reaches completion on the soul's entrance into beatitude.

The Punishments of Purgatory

To see the idea of a progressive punitive transformation at work, it is important to consider the nature of purgatorial punishments. We should recall at this point that the very nature of punishment is the infliction of an evil contrary to the will of the one being punished. This, as we saw, is the means of accomplishing retribution and restoring the equality of justice. Thus, we must consider the evils endured by the souls in purgatory and the way they contrast with the will of those being purified.

Here, however, we must already begin by qualifying this point. Given their basic conformity with the will of God in charity and their corresponding loving acceptance of his just judgment, the souls in purgatory undergo their punishments voluntarily.[41] They know that their suffering is required by divine justice, and they consent to it accordingly. Hence, what they undergo in purgatory does not contrast with their actual will, and we must look instead to their habitual or natural will as the seat of repugnance.

Classically, the two punishments to examine are the *poena damni* and the *poena sensus*.[42] They correspond to the two aspects of sin that we saw in the first chapter—*aversio a Deo* and *conversio ad creaturam*.[43] The *poena damni* punishes man insofar as he has turned away from God. The *poena sensus* punishes man for having turned improperly toward a created good.

---

[41] *Super Sent.*, lib. 4, dist. 21, q. 1, a. 1, qc. 4. Although Aquinas himself does not use the word, the subsequent tradition typically speaks about the experience of suffering in purgatory as "satispassion." This term recognizes that, although the punishment in purgatory is voluntary, it is neither meritorious nor active in the normal way that satisfaction during one's life is. It is something the souls voluntarily submit to rather than actively perform. Cf. Garrigou-Lagrange, *Life Everlasting*, 183.

[42] *Super Sent.*, lib. 4, dist. 21, q. 1, a. 1, qc. 3.

[43] *ST* Ia-IIae, q. 87, a. 4.

Poena Damni

For the souls in purgatory the *poena damni* (pain of loss) consists in the deprivation of the beatific vision.[44] More specifically, it is the *delay* of this vision, since they know they will soon be with the Lord. According to Garrigou-Lagrange this is the chief pain of purgatory.[45] Aquinas explains the reason for the intensity of their suffering in this way:

> For the more something is desired, the more troubling is its absence. And because the affection by which the highest good is desired in holy souls after this life is the most intense, since the affection is not held back by the weight of the body, and since the enjoyment of the highest good would have arrived by then had nothing impeded it; for these reasons they suffer extremely from this delay.[46]

He concludes from this thought that the punishment of purgatory "exceeds the greatest punishment of this life."[47] These souls' eager anticipation of heaven places them in great agony. They know that if it were not for their sins they would see God face-to-face in that very moment.

This punishment, though painful to the soul, is nevertheless voluntary, as I said above. The soul willingly endures the temporary separation because it is ordained by God in justice. As should be obvious, however, this deprivation does contrast with both the habitual and natural will of these souls. This double contrast is what gives the delay its truly punitive character. By their habitual charity the souls in purgatory long to be with the God whom they know and love. In like manner, the very nature of their will is made to possess the supreme Good, and to be deprived of him, even for a time, is a great loss. Thus, although the soul is primarily passive, voluntarily submitting to this delay allows the soul to restore the order of divine justice wounded by its sins.

It is helpful to recognize at the same time the fittingness of this form of punishment. As I mentioned above, the delay corresponds to the aspect of their sin that involved a turning away from the Lord—*aversio a Deo*. The

---

[44] *Super Sent.*, lib. 4, dist. 21, q. 1, a. 1, qc. 3

[45] Garrigou-Lagrange, *Life Everlasting*, 165.

[46] *Super Sent.*, lib. 4, dist. 21, q. 1, a. 1, qc. 3: "Quanto enim aliquid magis desideratur, tanto ejus absentia est molestior. Et quia affectus quo desideratur summum bonum, post hanc vitam in animabus sanctis est intensissimus, quia non retardatur affectus mole corporis, et etiam quia terminus fruendi summo bono jam advenisset, nisi aliquid impediret; ideo de tardatione maxime dolent."

[47] *Super Sent.*, lib. 4, dist. 21, q. 1, a. 1, qc. 3: "excedit maximam poenam hujus vitae."

fact that it is temporary fits with the imperfect (in the case of venial sin) or temporary (in the case of mortal sin now forgiven) nature of that aversion. Venial sin, we should recall, only includes a turning to the creature. In itself it implies no rejection of God as one's final end. It is a detour rather than a change in destination, as I suggested. Likewise, whatever mortal sins the souls in purgatory may have committed would have been forgiven. Only when there is true enmity with God in the *aversio* of unrepented mortal sin does man justly suffer an eternal *poena damni*.[48] Only then is the loss truly complete. When there is only a detour, as in the case of venial sin, the fitting punishment is delay.[49] The principle of charity which remains with the soul in venial sin or which returns to the soul with the forgiveness of mortal sin enables man to reach God as his final end. By that very charity he employs the proper means to reach that goal, even when those means involve the voluntary endurance of a just punishment for his sins. In other words, the disturbance of the order of justice caused by venial sin or forgiven mortal sins is reparable, and the punishment is fittingly temporal.[50]

Poena Sensus

In addition to this punishment, there must also be a punishment which corresponds to the *conversio ad creaturam*. Since this element is contained in all sin, both venial and mortal, it is properly applied in purgatory without the need to distinguish between a full or partial form of punishment, a distinction that is necessary in the case of the *poena damni*. This punishment for the *conversio ad creaturam* is typically called the *poena sensus* (pain of sense).

According to a classic and long-standing theological tradition in the West, the *poena sensus* is inflicted by means of true material fire. Given the similarities between the punishments of hell and purgatory (both have a retributive value corresponding to the disordered turn toward the creature), much of the theological reflection on the *poena sensus* by fire is connected to verses in the Scriptures that refer to the punishment of sinners and fallen angels in eternal fire.[51] The *locus classicus* for theological reflection on purgatorial fire, however, is St. Paul's first letter to the Corinthians:

---

[48] *SCG* III, cap. 144.
[49] *SCG* III, cap. 143.
[50] *ST* Ia-IIae, q. 87, a. 3, corp. and ad 4.
[51] Matt 25:41.

> For no other foundation can any one lay than that which is laid, which is Jesus Christ. Now if any one builds on the foundation with gold, silver, precious stones, wood, hay, straw—each man's work will become manifest; for the Day will disclose it, because it will be revealed with fire, and the fire will test what sort of work each one has done. If the work which any man has built on the foundation survives, he will receive a reward. If any man's work is burned up, he will suffer loss, though he himself will be saved, *but only as through fire.*[52]

According to the interpretation of Aquinas, a man places Christ as his foundation through faith informed by charity.[53] He is definitively united to Christ, and this ensures his final salvation. However, the fact that he builds with wood, hay, or straw describes his minor lapses and imperfections, his clinging inordinately to things that do not last. Aquinas writes, "He is drawn toward [created goods] more than he ought, so that he is kept back from the things of God by them; which is to sin venially."[54] These venial sins are then consumed by the fire of purgatory, and the man, though punished, is saved.[55] According to Aquinas, the central idea of purgatory is contained in this passage.

Nevertheless, many have wondered whether this and other passages really intend to speak about a material fire. It has been a topic of considerable debate in the history of the Church. At the Council of Florence, despite consensus among the Latin council fathers, the Church refrained from proclaiming this aspect of the Latin doctrine of purgatory out of concern for the Greeks who denied it.[56] Garrigou-Lagrange, however, takes the following position:

> After long discussions and wide historical researches on this particular point, it seems wise to conclude with St. Robert Bellarmine and Suarez as follows: "Although the existence of fire in purgatory

---

[52] 1 Cor 3:11–15 (emphasis mine).

[53] Thomas Aquinas, *Commentary on 1 Corinthians*, trans. Fabian Larcher [paragraphs 987–1046 trans. Daniel Keating; Commentary of Peter Tarentaise trans. Beth Mortensen], ed. and rev. the Aquinas Institute (Lander, WY: The Aquinas Institute, 2012), cap. 3, lec. 2, no. 155 (hereafter, *Super 1 ad Corinthios*).

[54] *Super 1 ad Corinthios*, cap. 3, lec. 2, n. 158: "afficitur tamen istis magis quam deberet, ita quod per haec retardatur ab his quae Dei sunt, quod est peccare venialiter."

[55] *Super Sent.*, d. 21, q. 1, a. 2, qc. 1.

[56] Garrigou-Lagrange, *Life Everlasting*, 173.

is less certain than that of fire in hell, the doctrine which admits a real fire in purgatory must be classified as a *sententia probabilissima*. Hence the contrary opinion is improbable."[57]

He reads the continued support for this position over the centuries in the West as a convincing sign of its truth. It is beyond my intention in this book, however, to take a firm stance on the issue. Principally, my intention has been to present a theory informed by the teaching of Aquinas who does hold strongly to the doctrine of a material fire in purgatory.[58] What is most illuminating, for our purposes, is recognizing the theological reasons that Aquinas advances for this theory.

As I alluded to above, the *poena sensus* corresponds to the turning toward the creature implicit in every sin. Aquinas explains:

> Those who sin against God are to be punished not only by forfeiting beatitude forever, but also by being subjected to some kind of pain. For punishment should be proportionate to fault, as we proved above. Now, when a man sins, his mind not only turns away from his last end, but also turns unduly to other things as ends. Therefore, the sinner should be punished not only by being debarred from his end, but *also by experiencing hurt from other things*.[59]

Fire, so the argument goes, generically represents all those created goods that man had turned to in his sin. In the wisdom of God's justice, then, the very object of man's sinful desire becomes the means of punishment. As the book of Wisdom teaches, "one is punished by the very things by which he sins."[60] The creation which drew man away from God now joins in God's work of restoring man to the right order of justice.

Since the soul is immaterial, however, the punishment cannot involve a corruption or alteration of the soul's nature.[61] The fire does not literally burn

---

[57] Garrigou-Lagrange, *Life Everlasting*, 173–174.

[58] *Super Sent.*, lib. 4, dist. 21, q. 1, a. 1, qc. 3.

[59] *SCG* III, cap. 145 (emphasis mine): "Non solum autem qui contra Deum peccant, puniendi sunt per hoc quod a beatitudine perpetuo excluduntur, sed per experimentum alicuius nocivi. Poena enim debet proportionaliter culpae respondere, ut supra ostensum est. In culpa autem non solum avertitur mens ab ultimo fine, sed etiam indebite convertitur in alia quasi in fines. Non solum ergo puniendus est qui peccat per hoc quod excludatur a fine, sed etiam per hoc quod ex aliis rebus sentiat nocumentum."

[60] Wis 11:16.

[61] *SCG* IV, cap. 90.

the soul. It is inconceivable that a material object could have that effect on a spiritual reality. Rather, "incorporeal substances suffer from the material fire by being coupled with it in some way."[62] By the force of divine power the soul is joined to the fire in such a way that the fire becomes a kind of prison for it. This union is contrary to the very nature of the will and is therefore punitive. As Aquinas explains, "it is contrary to the natural will of a spiritual substance that it be subject to a body, from which, according to the order of its nature, it should be free."[63] A man's will cannot help but detest this unnatural bondage. By patiently enduring this punishment, however, the soul gradually makes reparation to the divine justice his sin had offended.

A Transformative Poena Sensus

The temporary delay of the beatific vision and the punishment by material fire just described are the two punishments envisioned by Aquinas, and at face value it is difficult to see what transformative or rectifying power they might have. From this perspective, it is easy to understand how the debate about the two theories of purgatory developed. Even if the image of fire naturally evokes a sense of progressive purification, it is hard to imagine how that takes place under these conditions. At best, it would seem that the debt of punishment is the only thing consumed by each passing moment in purgatory.

Nevertheless, as Garrigou-Lagrange notes, there is evidence at least suggestive of a transforming finality to the punishments of purgatory in the writings of Aquinas. I think it is better to read such evidence as latent compatibilities—ideas that retain their principle meaning but make *even more* sense if we complement them with a transformative understanding of purgatory. In *De malo*, for example, Aquinas writes, "There is also a difference [between mortal and venial sin] regarding the liability to punishment, since one by mortal sin merits destructive punishment as an enemy, and one by venial sin merits *corrective punishment*."[64] Correction need not be limited either to this life or to the elimination of the *reatus poenae* in purgatory but

---

[62] *SCG* IV, cap. 90: "Patiuntur igitur ab igne corporeo substantiae incorporeae per modum alligationis cuiusdam."

[63] *SCG* IV, cap. 90: "Est autem contrarium naturali voluntati spiritualis substantiae ut corpori subdatur, a quo, secundum ordinem suae naturae, libera esse debet."

[64] *De malo*, q. 7, a. 11 (emphasis mine): "Ex parte etiam reatus poenae est differentia. Nam per peccatum mortale meretur, quasi inimicus effectus, poenam exterminantem; per peccatum vero veniale poenam corrigentem."

should also include moral transformation after death if such a position can be made intelligible.

The beginning of a way forward can be found in Aquinas's consideration of Gregory the Great's claim that the souls are punished by the very sight of the fire.[65] At face value, the idea contains a contradiction. Aquinas notes Aristotle's teaching that intellectual vision, in principle, is not a cause for sadness but rather delight. Vision perfects the one who sees. It is an enrichment of man's being. It seems difficult, therefore, to say that this intellectual illumination would be a punishment. There is no evil of being that is imposed. In his response Aquinas concedes that in itself the vision is not saddening, "since what is seen in no way could be understood to be contrary to the intellect, insofar as it is seen."[66] He admits, however, "intellectual vision can be saddening, inasmuch as what is seen is apprehended as harmful."[67] It is not *that* one sees but *what* one sees that makes the vision of fire punitive. In other words, although perfective in itself, it is punitive in an accidental way.

A similar idea is present in Aquinas's consideration of prayer as a work of satisfaction. Satisfaction, as we have seen, is at its core a work of retributive justice. Satisfaction, Aquinas argues, must therefore be accomplished by a penal work.[68] Man must deprive himself of something to restore the equality of justice. This is easy to account for in the traditional works of fasting and almsgiving, but the punitive nature of prayer is not immediately obvious. An objection states, "For a satisfactory work should be penal. But prayer holds no suffering, but pleasure, since it is a medicine against the sadness of punishment. This is why it says in James 5:13: *is anyone sad among you? Let him pray and praise God.* Therefore, it should not be counted among satisfactory works."[69]

Aquinas's response to this challenge is twofold. First, he admits a distinction between two kinds of prayer. Although some prayer, such as

---

[65] *Super Sent.*, lib. 4, dist. 44, q. 3, a. 3, qc. 3. Cf. Gregory the Great, *Dialogues*, lib. 4, cap. 30. Although Gregory and Aquinas are speaking about the fires of hell, there would be no difference with respect to the fire of purgatory.

[66] *Super Sent.*, lib. 4, dist. 44, q. 3, a. 3, qc. 3, ad 5: "cum illud quod videtur nullo modo intellectui possit esse contrarium, inquantum videtur."

[67] *Super Sent.*, lib. 4, dist. 44, q. 3, a. 3, qc. 3, ad 5: "Sed tamen visio intellectualis potest esse contristans, inquantum id quod videtur, apprehenditur ut nocivum."

[68] *Super Sent.*, lib. 4, dist. 15, q. 1, a. 4, qc. 1.

[69] *Super Sent.*, lib. 4, dist. 15, q. 1, a. 4, qc. 3, obj. 1: "Quia opus satisfactorium debet esse poenale. Sed oratio poenam non habet, cum sit contra poenae tristitiam medicina, sed delectationem; unde dicitur Jacob. 5, 13: *tristatur aliquis in vobis? Oret, et psallat.* Ergo non debet computari inter opera satisfactoria."

contemplative prayer, is entirely pleasant and not penal, another kind "is founded on grieving over sins; and this kind contains pain, and it is the part of satisfaction."[70] Second, however, in order to explain that all prayer is in some sense satisfactory, he notes that prayer, though pleasant to the soul, still involves a kind of affliction of the flesh.[71] Because of the bodily denial required, all prayer is penal.

The first half of his answer is the relevant part for our topic. Here, again, in the prayer of remorse we see a primarily perfective experience that nevertheless maintains a retributive value through the sorrow that adheres to it accidentally. Prayer, even when it involves meditating on one's sins, is good for the soul and cannot be considered a punishment in the strictest sense. It perfects and heals the soul. Nevertheless, because of the sorrow associated with it, it is a source of satisfaction when offered to divine justice.

These indications should give us greater confidence in accounting for a punishment in purgatory that is both retributive and transformative. In addition to the punishments described above, the soul in purgatory continues to receive the light of divine illumination that began at its separation from the body. Along with Aquinas's description of the separated soul's vision of the fire, we must say that fundamentally this enlightenment is good. The soul is perfected by seeing, no matter what it beholds. However, in his providence, God may choose to teach a given soul those things about reality and about himself that were contrasted by the man's former sins. The prideful man, for instance, might be compelled to consider the humility of Christ in the Incarnation. Such a vision would inevitably bring a combination of joy and sorrow—a sorrow that recalls the many times he himself failed to act this way. We can even imagine a series of these moments in which God lovingly but severely aids the soul in repenting of its own failings. The transformation that Bellarmine imagined at the moment of the particular judgment is echoed in this experience. As the soul endures the painful illumination, he continually makes acts of charity, loving those aspects of God that he failed to live up to in his life. Repeated acts of charity would slowly heal the habits, rendering the soul more and more perfect as the sorrow that accompanies them makes reparation to divine justice.

Again, it should be acknowledged that such an explicit and synthetic account cannot be found in the writings of Aquinas. However, it does fit with the principles I have articulated here and is fitting in a few ways. First,

---

[70] *Super Sent.*, lib. 4, dist. 15, q. 1, a. 4, qc. 3, ad 1: "alia est quae pro peccatis gemitus fundit; et talis habet poenam, et est satisfactionis pars."

[71] *Super Sent.*, lib. 4, dist. 15, q. 1, a. 4, qc. 3, ad 1.

it explains the theological purpose of the *poena sensus* fairly directly. The divine illumination does not contrast with the actual or natural will of the soul which delights in knowing God, but it does contrast in some way with the habitual will insofar as the soul is habitually averse to the experience of sorrow and as the evil dispositions still remain there, even if only in a minimal way. Something of the sinner's pride remains averse to Christ's humility (though obviously only in a limited sense). The material fire, as we saw, represented all created goods generically and, therefore, only contrasted with the will of man in a much more generic way. This punishment by illumination, however, contrasts in part with the very inherent effect of sin in his will. According to this account, "one is punished by the very things by which he sins" in an even more profound and direct way.[72] The residual inordinate affections, in other words, contribute directly to the punitive nature of this experience.

This kind of punishment also enables us to understand the demands of divine justice in a more intuitive way. In the last chapter I highlighted the distinction between punishments in the order of reason and punishments in the order of divine justice. One cannot be reduced to the other. Nevertheless, although it is clear that the fundamental concern in purgatory is the order of divine justice, a divine punishment that also roots out habitual evil dispositions maintains the link between the two orders of justice in a more harmonious way than does a punishment without transformation. Such a punishment would also help us to think about the "amount" of punishment needed to restore justice in purgatory. As we shall see in even more detail in the next chapter, it can be difficult to quantify this debt. What is required to make sufficient satisfaction? We have already seen that the punishments of the order of reason per se are not enough. How, then, could we understand the demands of justice without reducing justice to an arbitrary, external decree?

In his consideration of divine mercy, Aquinas notes that God always punishes man less than his faults deserve.[73] No man is required to bear the true penalty for his sins. While this reality impedes us from answering the speculative question of man's objective obligation prior to God's merciful dispensation, it does permit us to see a certain flexibility in God's demand for just retribution. Although he does not deny the requirements of justice, in his wisdom he may adapt them to a given situation. In light of the harmony between the punishments of reason and divine justice suggested by the vision of transformative punishment, it is possible to imagine that

---

[72] Wis 11:16.
[73] *Super Sent.*, lib. 4, dist. 46, q. 2, a. 2, qc. 1, ad 1.

by God's sapiential dispensation the "amount" of punishment needed to satisfy divine justice in purgatory is coordinated with the time required to painfully root out the evil dispositions. It is within his power and merciful governance of man, in other words, to orchestrate divine justice in view of a plenary restoration of man's habitual moral dispositions so that the scope of the two converge on a common mean. What is required to restore us is also what is owed to divine justice, even though the two remain logically irreducible. It does not have to be this way, but God may ordain it so.

As I suggested above, if this account is true, it also helps us to find deeper intelligibility in certain ideas of Aquinas, aspects of his own doctrine that he may not have unpacked. As I noted above, he argues that the length of time in purgatory corresponds to the rootedness of sin. In light of what I have suggested the following claim becomes more profound:

> It should be said that some venial sins adhere more than others, according as the affections are more inclined to them and are fixed upon them more strongly. And because the ones that adhere more take longer to purify, for this reason some people are tormented in purgatory longer than others, according as their affections were more steeped in venial sins.[74]

More than simply being a metric of divine justice, in a transformative vision of purgatory the rootedness of man's imperfect affections is intrinsically related to the experience of punishment. A given soul may be detained longer than another because it requires more contrary acts of love to root out its residual evil dispositions. The process is tailored to each individual soul.

This insight accords with Aquinas's affirmation that it is the charity of the souls in purgatory that determines the healing nature of their punishment. He writes:

> Such punishments derive their cleansing power from the condition of those who suffer them. For the souls in purgatory have charity, by which their wills are conformed to the divine will; it is owing to this charity that the punishments they suffer avail them for cleansing.

---

[74] *Super Sent.*, lib. 4, dist. 21, q. 1, a. 3, qc. 3: "Ad tertiam quaestionem dicendum, quod quaedam venialia sunt majoris adhaerentiae quam alia, secundum quod affectus magis ad ea inclinatur, et fortius in eis figitur: et quia ea quae sunt majoris adhaerentiae, tardius purgantur, ideo quidam in Purgatorio diutius quam alii torquentur, secundum quod affectus eorum ad venialia fuit magis immersus."

This is why punishment has no cleansing force in those who lack charity, such as the damned.[75]

Most likely, Aquinas principally thinks of cleansing with reference to the satisfaction of the *reatus poenae*. Charity is what ensures that the souls only undergo a temporary punishment. However, within a transformative vision, it is also the charity of those in purgatory that allows their punishment to rectify the residual evil dispositions. Their charity enables them to make the very acts of love that wear away these imperfections. In contrast, even if the damned were permitted to receive similar divine illuminations, they could only despise them and remain averse.

CHALLENGES

Despite what has been said, there are a few passages from Aquinas that present potential challenges to the vision I articulated. Given the controversial nature of the question and my claim that nothing in Aquinas definitively contradicts the position, it is essential to consider these texts. Rather than undermining the current argument, however, I believe they instead provide helpful clarifications that underscore what this account does *not* mean to propose.

In the first text to consider, Aquinas claims that the souls in purgatory gain nothing from their punishments.[76] As I mentioned above, these souls voluntarily submit to their punitive suffering. However, Aquinas notes that punishment may be voluntary in two ways. In the first, the punishment is the direct means of acquiring some good.[77] This is the case in earthly satisfaction or in martyrdom. We *want* to do these things because of the good we obtain. The other way punishment is voluntary is when no good comes to us by it, and yet we know that we cannot obtain the good desired by any other means.[78] The examples Aquinas gives for this kind of voluntary punishment are natural death and purgatory. Neither of these directly causes good but is voluntarily endured only because of some good that awaits the souls on the

---

[75] *Compendium theologiae*, lib. 1, cap. 182: "Habent autem istae poenae quod sint purgatoriae ex conditione eorum qui eas patiuntur, in quibus est caritas per quam voluntatem suam divinae voluntati conformant; ex cuius caritatis virtute poenae quas patiuntur, eis ad purgationem prosunt: unde in his qui sine caritate sunt, sicut in damnatis."

[76] *Super Sent.*, lib. 4, dist. 21, q. 1, a. 1, qc. 4.

[77] *Super Sent.*, lib. 4, dist. 21, q. 1, a. 1, qc. 4.

[78] *Super Sent.*, lib. 4, dist. 21, q. 1, a. 1, qc. 4.

other side. Aquinas notes that people long to be free of this second kind of voluntary punishment as quickly as possible.

At face value this passage presents a difficulty for a transformative vision of purgatory. Is not this moral rectification something that the souls gain by their submission to punishment? Here it is important to remember that, in a real sense, souls are not better off for having to go to purgatory. If this were the case, the prayers of the Church for a speedy delivery from purgatory would be detrimental to the souls there. Time in purgatory is never to one's credit. The transformative dimension of purgatory, as I have articulated it, does not give the soul anything it could not gain from God's gratuitous healing and the perfective effects of the beatific vision. The transformative and meritorious value of earthly suffering which allows the saints to reach the heights of heroic virtue is not applicable in purgatory. No one becomes a hero in purgatory. As we have seen, merit is no longer possible after death, and the transformative aspect of punishment in purgatory is primarily one of moral rectification rather than of progress in charity.

A similar challenge comes from *De malo*. In question seven, article eleven, Aquinas clarifies that the movement of love in purgatory which remits the guilt of venial sin nevertheless does not diminish or decrease the punishment to be endured.[79] During this life, this dynamic is possible. An intense act of love on earth can merit the release from all debt to divine justice.[80] However, as we have seen, merit is no longer possible after this life, and so neither are these acts of love sufficient to remit the *reatus poenae*.

However, did not the transformative vision proposed above suggest that the movements of love slowly restored the equality of justice? Not exactly. It is important to remember the irreducibility of the two aspects of the experience. According to the transformative account of purgatory presented here, the movements of love in purgatory are *effective* for the rectification of evil dispositions but are not *meritorious* for the remission of temporal punishment. The satisfaction of the *reatus poenae* is only accomplished in purgatory by the endurance of a sufficient punishment. In other words, only the punitive dimension of the experience fulfills the demand of divine justice, and it is the sorrow and repentance caused by the divine illumination that form that indispensable punitive element. The act of love which accompanies that vision has a distinct finality: the rectification of the habits. The two must be seen distinctly even in their coordination.

This nuance can be difficult for us to discern because of the meritorious

---

[79] *De malo*, q. 7, a. 11.

[80] *De malo*, q. 7, a. 11; *Compendium theologiae*, lib. 1, cap. 182.

dimension of satisfaction during this life that I highlighted in the last chapter. On earth, the intensity of love in the voluntary acceptance of penance often brings more to the soul in grace than the act alone is strictly sufficient to obtain. As I mentioned, a particularly intense love can eliminate the need for punishment. However, in purgatory, where there is no further possibility of merit, the punitive aspect, even though voluntary, does not grant a new outpouring of grace. The greater love of a particular soul does not permit it to move through purgatory more quickly. Each must simply endure the fitting punishment according to God's just sentence. This point gives us all the greater motivation to perform our penance now while we have the chance.

The Scriptum *Passage*

Finally, as I mentioned above, there is one passage in Aquinas's commentary on the *Sentences* that does contradict the proposal of this chapter. Nevertheless, I believe it can be shown that this passage reflects an early position of Aquinas that changed in a significant way in his later writings.

In this text, he considers the opinion of those who claim that no venial sin needs to be forgiven after this life because death destroys concupiscence and ipso facto subjects the powers of the soul to grace.[81] Any remaining venial sin, so the argument claims, is removed by this automatic reordering of the soul.

Aquinas, however, rejects the argument. He notes that death does not remove concupiscence but only inhibits it from acting. He writes:

> Now as to the argument for this opinion, its worthlessness is apparent, for bodily defect, such as there is at the end of life, does not remove or diminish the corruption of concupiscence as to its root, but as to its act, as is seen even in those who are extremely weakened. Nor again does it calm the powers of the soul, so that they are subject to grace, for the tranquility of the powers and their subjection to grace is when the lower powers obey the higher ones that *delight in the law of God* (Rom 7:22).[82]

---

[81] *Super Sent.*, lib. 4, dist. 21, q. 1, a. 3, qc. 1.

[82] *Super Sent.*, lib. 4, dist. 21, q. 1, a. 3, qc. 1: "Quantum ad causam autem frivola apparet; quia defectus corporalis, qualis est in ultimo vitae, non aufert concupiscentiae corruptionem vel diminuit, quantum ad radicem, sed quantum ad actum; sicut patet etiam de illis qui graviter infirmantur. Nec iterum tranquillat potentias animae, ut eas gratiae subjiciat; quia tranquillitas potentiarum et subjectio earum ad gratiam est, quando inferiores vires obediunt superioribus, quae legi Dei condelectantur."

In this short section he affirms two major principles that seem to suggest the need for the rectification of evil dispositions. First, he acknowledges that the powers of the soul are not destroyed by death, and second, in accordance with this claim, he shows that death does not calm those powers of the soul or subject them to grace.

The problematic phrase follows, however. Such a subjection of the lower powers to the higher ones, he explains, "cannot exist in that state, since the act of either one is impeded."[83] Although his argument implied the need for rectification, here he argues that this kind of a transformation cannot take place in purgatory. Because the powers are impeded in their operation, they cannot be harmonized. If this reading is correct, it provides additional confirmation of the idea that he considered the beatific vision itself as perfective of the soul.

That being said, as I suggested, there is a contradiction in Aquinas's argument here with an aspect of his mature position. In this particular passage the subjection of the powers is tangential to the main issue, the forgiveness of venial sins. His point in the argument I presented is only to show that the guilt of some venial sins may remain in the soul after death. In this *quaestiuncula* he concludes by arguing that venial sins are forgiven after death for those who die with grace. He writes, "venial sin in someone who dies with grace is remitted after this life by the fire of purgatory, for that punishment, which is voluntary in a certain way, will have the power by virtue of grace of expiating every fault that can exist together with grace."[84] Here he claims that it is the punishment itself that forgives sins. The fire of purgatory, in other words, has the power of expiating fault.

Nevertheless, as we have seen, this is not his claim in the more mature *De malo*. In his response to objection nine of question seven, article eleven of that work, Aquinas states, "But regarding moral fault, punishment does not remit venial sin insofar as one actually undergoes punishment, since punishment is not meritorious."[85] Rather, "the power of graces remits venial sin in purgatory regarding moral fault both as grace is habitual . . . and as

---

[83] *Super Sent.*, lib. 4, dist. 21, q. 1, a. 3, qc. 1: "quod in statu illo esse non potest, cum actus utrarumque impediatur."

[84] *Super Sent.*, lib. 4, dist. 21, q. 1, a. 3, qc. 1: "culpa venialis in eo qui cum gratia decedit, post hanc vitam dimittitur per ignem Purgatorium; quia poena illa aliqualiter voluntaria, virtute gratiae habebit vim expiandi culpam omnem quae simul cum gratia stare potest."

[85] *De malo*, q. 7, a. 11, ad 9: "sed quantum ad culpam non remittitur per poenam neque secundum quod actu sustinetur, quia non est meritoria."

grace issues in *an act of charity* detesting venial sin."[86] Here, it is not the punishment but the act of love that brings forgiveness.[87]

This change also shows us the key development in Aquinas's thought. In the *Scriptum*, punishment had to forgive venial sin because it was the only means available. There he claimed that neither the lower powers *nor the higher powers* were active—"the act of either one is impeded."[88] In *De malo*, however, his account presumes that the higher powers are still operative. As we have seen, because the higher powers do not intrinsically depend upon material organs, they remain active after death, though in a different mode. Aquinas, therefore, now attributes forgiveness to the fervent act of charity of the will of the separated soul, in accordance with the way that venial sin is ordinarily forgiven. This act of love, as I have argued, can also account for the rectification of the residual evil dispositions.

This passage does, however, yet again help us to clarify the precise nature of the rectification that takes place according to the transformative account presented here. Because the sense powers have ceased to exist in act,[89] any purgatorial rectification would apply only to the truly spiritual powers.[90] A complete transformation that fully included the sensory powers and their submission to the higher powers would have to wait until the resurrection of the body. That being said, it would be inaccurate to imagine that this qualification represents an imperfection in the healing process. Because the sense powers merely exist *in radice* (in root) in the separated soul, whatever imperfections cannot be healed there do not inhibit the soul's enjoyment of beatitude in any way. In fact, like the powers themselves, the residual evil dispositions of the sense faculties no longer exist in act. When, therefore, the bodies of the blessed rise they will automatically share in the glory and

---

[86] *De malo*, q. 7, a. 11, ad 9 (emphasis mine): "Remittitur ergo in Purgatorio veniale quantum ad culpam virtute gratiae, non solum secundum quod est in habitu, quia sic compatitur veniale peccatum, sed prout exit in actum caritatis detestantis veniale peccatum."

[87] The English Province translation of *ST* Supp. App. 1, q. 2, a. 4. (which reproduces the relevant section from the *Scriptum* concerning the expiatory effect of Purgatorial fire), notes this development in Aquinas's thought. Thomas Aquinas, *Summa theologica*, English Province Translation (New York: Benziger Brothers, 1947).

[88] *Super Sent.*, lib. 4, dist. 21, q. 1, a. 3, qc. 1: "actus utrarumque impediatur."

[89] *De anima*, q. 19.

[90] Cf. Garrigou-Lagrange, *Life Everlasting*, 186. Here Garrigou-Lagrange argues that this rectification only takes place in the purely spiritual faculties. Thus, the separated soul can acquire prudence and justice but not chastity, for instance. That being said, given that the will is the source of all activity and that all virtues are interconnected, it seems possible that some basic perfection could flow from the will's act of charity into the latent sense powers of the soul in such a way that some seminal rectification takes place. Nevertheless, even with Garrigou-Lagrange's restriction, the basic argument still stands.

perfection that the separated soul has since obtained. In the meantime, a true and thorough healing of the soul does take place in purgatory as the residual evil dispositions of the spiritual faculties are wiped away by each repeated act of love.

Aquinas does not consider this possibility in the passage in question, however, because at that time he seems to have thought that these higher powers were also inactive. Having seen that Aquinas abandons this position later and that he does not reevaluate the relevant argument (it was, as I said, tangential even in the *Scriptum* passage), the rectification of the moral habits of the will after death in Aquinas's mature thought remains an open question. Nevertheless, I believe the presentation I have given here is a plausible account of how Aquinas himself might have considered the issue in light of his definitive positions.

CONCLUSION

The analysis of this chapter has highlighted the complexity and difficulty of the question of moral transformation in purgatory. It is undeniable that many Catholics, especially today, understand purgatory in these terms, but finding theological support in the tradition has not always been easy. Aquinas himself is suggestive but inconclusive, and Bellarmine and Suarez both exerted significant influence in the opposite direction. However, in more recent times Garrigou-Lagrange and John Paul II have challenged us to reconsider the issue. While I still maintain that the proposal of this chapter is original and, consequently, provisional, it is nevertheless an attempt to follow this impetus and bring Aquinas into the conversation in a more explicit and studied way.

As we have seen, his teaching and principles provide us with helpful conceptual tools. In particular, the simultaneously perfective and punitive nature of both the vision of fire and the prayer of contrition suggests the possibility of a transformative punishment. When applied to purgatory, the effect of divine illumination on the residual evil dispositions in the spiritual powers harmonizes well with this perspective. It allows us to maintain the primacy of the retributive finality of purgatory while incorporating a genuine account of moral healing. The punishment thus described points to the beauty and wisdom that is characteristic of all of God's works. He heals at the very place where the sin occurred. As a healing balm stings an open wound, the brilliance of God's light calls attention to our past sins, causing deep and genuine transformative sorrow. The pain, however, is not an unfortunate accident. The restoration of justice demands it be done this way. Nevertheless, it is not the justice of a cold and exacting despot but of a loving and tender Father.

It is worth mentioning that this depiction of purgatory is similar to the position of "some recent theologians" presented by Benedict XVI in *Spe Salvi*:

> Some recent theologians are of the opinion that the fire which both burns and saves is Christ himself, the Judge and Saviour. The encounter with him is the decisive act of judgement. Before his gaze all falsehood melts away. *This encounter with him, as it burns us, transforms and frees us, allowing us to become truly ourselves.* All that we build during our lives can prove to be mere straw, pure bluster, and it collapses. Yet in the pain of this encounter, when the impurity and sickness of our lives become evident to us, there lies salvation. *His gaze, the touch of his heart heals us through an undeniably painful transformation "as through fire."* But it is a blessed pain, in which the holy power of his love sears through us like a flame, enabling us to become totally ourselves and thus totally of God. In this way the inter-relation between justice and grace also becomes clear: the way we live our lives is not immaterial, but our defilement does not stain us for ever if we have at least continued to reach out towards Christ, towards truth and towards love. Indeed, it has already been burned away through Christ's Passion. At the moment of judgement we experience and we absorb the overwhelming power of his love over all the evil in the world and in ourselves. The pain of love becomes our salvation and our joy. It is clear that we cannot calculate the "duration" of this transforming burning in terms of the chronological measurements of this world. The transforming "moment" of this encounter eludes earthly time-reckoning—it is the heart's time, it is the time of "passage" to communion with God in the Body of Christ. The judgement of God is hope, both because it is justice and because it is grace. If it were merely grace, making all earthly things cease to matter, God would still owe us an answer to the question about justice—the crucial question that we ask of history and of God. If it were merely justice, in the end it could bring only fear to us all. The incarnation of God in Christ has so closely linked the two together—judgement and grace—that justice is firmly established: we all work out our salvation "with fear and trembling" (*Phil* 2:12). Nevertheless grace allows us all to

hope, and to go trustfully to meet the Judge whom we know as our "advocate," or *parakletos* (cf. *1 Jn* 2:1).[91]

Although the two descriptions come from distinct theological schools, the similarities are striking. The principal differences between this description and the one that I have presented here are that my position emphasizes more specifically the punitive nature of the punishment (although the text here mentions justice) and that the encounter that I describe with God in purgatory is more generically "divine illumination" (following the lead of Aquinas) rather than what seems to be the operation of the sacred humanity of Christ in this text. That being said, the two accounts are certainly compatible and the direction of theological exploration is harmonious. Nevertheless, it would require more work to unpack exactly how the divine illumination of the souls in purgatory might take place instrumentally through the sacred humanity of Christ, something that Aquinas does not appear to consider.

---

[91] Benedict XVI, Encyclical Letter *Spe Salvi* (November 30, 2007), §47, accessed March 24, 2023, https://www.vatican.va/content/benedict-xvi/en/encyclicals/documents/hf_ben-xvi_enc_20071130_spe-salvi.html (emphasis mine).

CHAPTER V

Personal Satisfaction in This Life

THE ANALYSIS OF THE PREVIOUS CHAPTERS completes the Thomistic account of purgatory that I have sought to present in this book. We have seen that Aquinas's principles permit us to describe a medicinal punishment after death that simultaneously heals the soul's residual evil dispositions and restores the equality of justice. This vision allows us to understand both the wisdom and beauty at work in divine providence while preserving the authentic, traditional understanding of temporal punishment and the *reatus poenae*. It is my hope that this account somewhat tempers the image of a ruthless and vengeful God that is often evoked by the appeal to these classic notions.

Nevertheless, such a presentation should not obscure the sobering reality. The endurance of temporal punishment in purgatory, though joyful, will be an immensely agonizing experience. By an intuitive principle, we can say that it will certainly be more painful than whatever discomfort we might have experienced on earth simply by avoiding sin in the first place. No one can hedge his bets on a lighter burden in purgatory. Rather, in the words of St. Paul, "now is the acceptable time . . . now is the day of salvation."[1] For reasons that I will discuss in this chapter and the next, it is much better to begin making satisfaction for our sins during this life. As we will see, such great resources are at man's disposal that if he is earnest and committed to the cause of restoring justice, he can do much to mitigate the need for purgatory and will likely grow in holiness and charity in the process.

In this vein, the purpose of this chapter is to understand the nature and shape of personal satisfaction in this life now that we have properly understood the centrality of temporal punishment in purgatory. Before considering personal satisfaction, however, we cannot neglect to recall the

---

[1] 2 Cor 6:2.

satisfaction made for us by Christ. This reality serves as the essential foundation for considering all subsequent personal satisfactory works. With this groundwork in place, we will then be able to understand the real but subordinate nature of personal satisfaction. I will begin from a sacramental perspective, but we will see that this structure flows quite naturally into the extra-sacramental forms of satisfaction as well, the chief of which is martyrdom. As we will see at every stage of the analysis, the centrality of charity repeatedly comes to the fore. From the satisfaction offered by Christ to the satisfactory works that we undertake in union with him, it is ultimately the charity that informs these actions that gives them their greatest value, even as they maintain an irreducible punitive or retributive finality. As should not be surprising, the harmony between the perfective and retributive elements of human purification in purgatory is all the more present in the satisfactory works performed by the living.

The Satisfaction of Christ

Although the focus of this chapter is the personal satisfaction of the faithful for sins committed after baptism, it is important to recall the foundational and central role of Christ in this process. He is the one, after all, who has made perfect satisfaction for our sins in his Passion and death. Were we to forget this truth, we would justly be subject to the reproach of Calvin who, as we saw, accused Catholics of seeking satisfaction outside of Christ himself. To do so would be to deny both the significance of the Incarnation and Christ's unique status as the universal savior of mankind. He alone is, ultimately, the one who makes perfect satisfaction. As the book of Hebrews teaches, "by a single offering he has perfected for all time those who are sanctified."[2]

Because he was guilty of no sin, Christ had no need to make satisfaction for himself. We can speak of no *reatus poenae* with respect to Christ in a proper personal sense. Nevertheless, by virtue of the Incarnation, Christ took upon himself our human condition. In the enigmatic words of St. Paul, "For our sake he made him to be sin who knew no sin, so that in him we might become the righteousness of God."[3] By the Incarnation, in other words, Christ forged a solidarity with all men that allowed him to make satisfaction for our sins.

Beyond the solidarity established, however, the Incarnation was also necessary for another reason. The requisite satisfaction that man owes to

---

[2] Heb 10:14.
[3] 2 Cor 5:21.

God exceeds mere human ability. Man's debt of punishment is quasi-infinite. As Romanus Cessario explains:

> The offense for which [satisfaction] is made touches the infinite in three ways: first, the infinite character of the divine majesty that is offended; second, the infinite dimension of the good from which sinful man is separated by original sin, namely, the good of God himself; and lastly, the unlimited, even infinite, potential of the human nature which is being restored.[4]

However, since no creature is capable of making this infinite satisfaction, divine intervention is required. It is in virtue of the divine personhood of Christ and the grace that flows from it, therefore, that his satisfactory work possesses the infinite value necessary for addressing the infinity of man's debt. Although the severity of his suffering certainly gives the Passion a great satisfactory value, Aquinas more fundamentally points to the dignity of Christ's person and the love with which he patiently endured his sufferings as the true reasons for the exceeding worth of his self-offering.[5]

Christ is thus in an exclusive position to be able to make reparation to divine justice. He not only possesses the necessary solidarity with all men but is also uniquely capable of repairing the infinite offence of each and every human sin. By laying down his life on Calvary, he accomplished that goal and in one sacrifice did enough to make perfect and infinite satisfaction for all men.

Sacramental Sharing in Christ's Satisfaction

The satisfaction won for us by Christ first enters man's life in the sacrament of baptism. This is the primary means for the remission of both temporal and eternal punishment. This sacrament of spiritual regeneration remits all of the punishment due to sin. As was mentioned above, Aquinas explains that at the moment of baptism the infinite satisfaction of Christ's Passion is applied perfectly to the new Christian "just as if he himself had offered sufficient satisfaction for all his sins."[6] It is a complete and total gift in accor-

---

[4] Romanus Cessario, *The Godly Image: Christian Satisfaction in Aquinas* (Washington, DC: The Catholic University of America Press, 2020), 99.

[5] *ST* IIIa, q. 48, a. 2. *SCG* IV, cap. 55. For more on the relationship between charity and the satisfaction offered by Christ, see Daria Spezzano, "'Be Imitators of God' (Eph 5:1): Aquinas on Charity and Satisfaction," *Nova et Vetera* 15, no. 2 (2017): 615–51.

[6] *ST* IIIa, q. 69, a. 2: "ac si ipse sufficienter satisfecisset pro omnibus peccatis suis."

dance with the beginning of a radically new life. However, as we also saw, the situation is different for sins forgiven after baptism. For postbaptismal sins, man himself must share in the work of satisfaction.

This distinction is best explained by Aquinas's presentation of the sacraments in book four of the *Summa contra Gentiles*. There, Aquinas presents the sacrament of penance in light of an analogy based on natural life.[7] In the spiritual life of man, the sacrament of penance is analogous to natural healing. Unlike generation, which proceeds entirely from without (Aquinas sees an analogy with baptism here), most forms of natural healing involve the coordination of forces both inside and outside the patient. Medical doctors, for instance, must rely on and assist the natural recuperative power of the body. Something similar takes place in the sacrament of penance. Although the gracious gift of God is required, the sacrament works by assisting man in personally performing the necessary actions. Man's cooperation plays a much more significant role in penance than in baptism. In technical terms, the actions of the penitent compose the matter of the sacrament of penance. The grace of the sacrament then works to enable, aid, and direct the penitent's own actions to their proper end so that he can fully recover from the evil of sin. What is freely given to man in the sacrament of baptism is elicited from man in the sacrament of penance. To put it simply, in the sacrament of penance man must cooperate in his own healing—while still relying on the grace of Christ—in order to overcome the evil of sin.

As we saw in chapter one, the evil of sin is threefold: guilt, evil dispositions, and the *reatus poenae*. Principally, sin involves a turning away from God and a turning toward the creature. It is a defect in the actual orientation of the will. This disordering is guilt (*reatus culpae*) properly speaking and is overcome by a reordering of one's life to God, either through a new infusion of charity or, in the case of venial sin, by an act of fervor in virtue of the charity already habitually possessed. Nevertheless, evil dispositions and the *reatus poenae* remain as distinct consequences of sin that must be addressed in the process of man's plenary restoration. The constitutive parts of the sacrament of penance (contrition, confession, and satisfaction) are thus coordinated to effectively address each of these three evils.[8]

Contrition

The actual disorder of the will (guilt) is rectified by the contrition of the penitent. According to Aquinas, contrition is a grieving for sin committed

---

[7] *SCG* IV, cap. 72.
[8] *SCG* IV, cap. 72.

and a resolve not to commit it again.[9] It is a spiritual sorrow for past sins that includes a desire to reorient one's will to God. It is important to recognize, however, that this sorrow exists on a spectrum. On the one hand, it is possible to imagine a kind of natural sorrow for sin motivated merely by the negative consequences of sin. On the other hand, many great saints of the Church have witnessed to the incredible depths that this sorrow can reach when informed by perfect charity. Such a recognition leads to the classic theological dilemma of the distinction between attrition and contrition. The *Catechism of the Catholic Church* distinguishes the two as imperfect and perfect sorrow for sin, respectively.[10]

Nearly all theologians agree that perfect contrition is a reordering of the soul to God as one's final end motivated by a gratuitous infusion of sanctifying grace and the theological virtue of charity. It always includes the resolve to confess one's sins and to perform the requisite penance, since these are indispensable parts of the sacramental economy instituted by Christ.[11] Strictly speaking, however, this perfect contrition already includes the restoration of the habitual love of God as one's final end, even when performed outside of the sacrament.

In contrast, attrition is meant to describe an imperfect sorrow for one's sins that is born in some sense from a fear of damnation and the other penalties of sin but that is nevertheless sufficient for the reception of the sacrament of penance.[12] Here, however, theological opinions vary. Some have argued that a purely natural sorrow is sufficient, while others have questioned the legitimacy of the concept of attrition altogether.[13] The latter position appropriately recognizes the need for a supernatural motive in the reception of the sacraments. However, by rejecting the sufficiency of an imperfect contrition that is not already motivated by habitual charity, one comes to the absurd conclusion that the sinner is only ever justified before the sacrament of penance and never in virtue of the grace of the sacrament itself.

The challenge lies in the principle that sorrow only ever follows from an antecedent love. One grieves over the absence of the beloved. Without love, therefore, there can be no sorrow. The man in a state of sin, however, by definition, lacks charity. How, then, can he elicit a sorrow for sin based on

---

9 *ST* IIIa, q. 90, a. 2.

10 CCC, §§1451–53.

11 CCC, §1452.

12 CCC, 1453. The Thomist school holds that when the penitent comes to the sacrament of penance with attrition only, the sacrament causes perfect contrition through the infusion of grace. Colman E. O'Neill, *Meeting Christ in the Sacraments*, rev. ed. Romanus Cessario (New York: Alba House, 1991), 259.

13 Garrigou-Lagrange, *Reality*, 180.

the love of God? In response to this difficulty, Garrigou-Lagrange expresses a common position of the Thomistic school in asserting the possibility of a benevolent love of God prompted by actual grace that does not yet include the stable divine friendship of habitual charity.[14] This imperfect love is analogous to the mutual benevolence that precedes and prepares for genuine friendship, and it enables the sorrow of attrition requisite for receiving the grace of sacramental absolution. Only with the reception of this sacramental grace is man fully restored to habitual friendship with God in charity. This important theological distinction is supported by the *Catechism* in its affirmation that attrition is "also a gift of God, a prompting of the Holy Spirit."[15] This short line confirms the principle that even imperfect sorrow for sin must be motivated by a love that can only come from God himself.

The distinction between contrition and attrition thus defended preserves the intuition that the intensity of contrition varies from person to person. The sorrow of some, though sufficient, remains weak, while others come to the sacrament marked by a spirit of a humble and profound compunction. As we will see below, the quality of the contrition will have a role to play in the determination of the *reatus poenae*. For now it is sufficient to note that with the help of the sacrament, even attrition is sufficient to allow the sinner to overcome his guilt, which is the first and principal evil of sin.

Confession and Satisfaction

The remaining two parts of the sacrament of penance can be viewed together because they both aim at the healing of the other two evils of sin, evil dispositions and the *reatus poenae*. Although, as we have seen, there has been reason to debate the transformative nature of purgatorial punishments, the medicinal quality of the satisfaction imposed in the sacrament of penance is uncontroversial. The penitent is in need of transformation, and the sacrament of penance is a privileged means for attaining this goal.

The confession of sin precedes the work of satisfaction and serves to link it with the penitent's contrition. The explicit, external manifestation of the object of his sorrow gives the action its sacramental quality. The sacraments by their very nature require this kind of sensory instantiation. In addition, this action also manifests the submission of the penitent to Christ through the ordained minister.[16] It is a humble recognition that the grace

---

[14] Garrigou-Lagrange, *Reality*, 180.

[15] CCC, §1453.

[16] *SCG* IV, cap. 72.

necessary for forgiveness comes through the sacred humanity of Christ and the sacramental means instituted by him.

At the same time, the fact that the confession enables the priest to accurately judge the state of the penitent's soul is of central importance for Aquinas.[17] This judgment is not one of condemnation or reproof, however, but rather one of mercy. Just as the doctor needs to know the illness in order to prescribe the appropriate medicine, so too does the priest need to know the sin in order to apply a fitting remedy. As Aquinas explains, "the penitent who comes to Christ to be healed must look to Christ for the assessment of the punishment, and Christ prescribes the remedy through his minister, as he does in the other sacraments. No one, however, can judge sins of which he is not informed. Consequently, it was necessary to institute confession as the second part of this sacrament."[18]

From the context of this text it is clear that the penance imposed by the priest ought to aim at both the healing of the soul's dispositions and the satisfaction of temporal punishment.[19] As I have been arguing, even when the retributive dimension of punishment is coordinated and harmonized with the medicinal, it does not lose its own inherent logic. Thus, in assigning a proper penance, the priest should not only think of remedying the interior wounds of sin but must also take account of the debt to divine justice.[20]

In this context, the question naturally arises, "what is sufficient satisfaction?" How much penance must man perform? As I hinted at in the last chapter, it can be difficult to "quantify" the debt of punishment that a man owes for past sins. We have no direct access to God's judgment. In addition, we can have a reasonable hope in the gracious gentleness of divine mercy that would attenuate the precision of such a measurement even if measuring were

---

[17] SCG IV, cap. 72.

[18] SCG IV, cap. 72: "oportet quod poenitens, qui se Christo sanandum commisit, Christi iudicium in taxatione poenae expectet: quod quidem per suos ministros exhibet Christus, sicut et cetera sacramenta. Nullus autem potest iudicare de culpis quas ignorat. Necessarium igitur fuit confessionem institui, quasi secundam partem huius sacramenti."

[19] Again, there is both harmony and distinction between the two. Such a realization, however, places a great burden upon the priest. He not only needs to discern and understand the dynamics of virtue and vice in a vast array of diverse people but must also have an appreciation for the demands of divine justice. Although there is much that could be said about applying an appropriate penance in order to aid the soul in its fight against sin in the future, this consideration is beyond the scope of this book. Our present concern is temporal punishment itself.

[20] In Super Sent., lib. 4, dist. 15, q. 1, a. 1, qc. 3, ad 4, Aquinas explains that the medicinal aspect of satisfactory works during this life has a primacy over the retributive aspect. In practice, it is always important to keep this in mind. However, the nature of our investigation justifies the focus of this chapter on temporal punishment itself.

possible. Nevertheless, at first glance, there must be some means available at least to approximate a kind of metric, even if only a relative one. If the confessor is to assign an *appropriate* penance, he must have some means for evaluating the demands of divine justice in a given case.

The work of approximation can gain some initial foundation by a consideration of the particular nature of the justice involved in the Christian's personal satisfaction. Aquinas explains, "the mean of justice is taken according to the equalizing of one thing to another in a certain proportion."[21] To put it simply, justice aims at a kind of equality. However, in the case of personal satisfaction made by the faithful to God, no strict equality is possible. Christ has made such perfect satisfaction for us, but, as we have seen, man himself could never accomplish this task. Nevertheless, this impossibility does not preclude all forms of justice.

Within certain relationships, justice does not demand an "equality of quantity," as just described, but rather an "equality of proportion."[22] The latter describes the equality that governs the devotion and honor that children owe their parents or the worship due to God, for example. In these cases, a strict equality of quantity is not possible. However, Aquinas beautifully explains that, in these cases, "it is enough that a man render what he can: for friendship does not require an equivalent except according as it is possible."[23] As implied by this passage, Aquinas conceives the friendship implicit in these relationships as the appropriate grounding for the equality of proportion. Due to their affective union with their children, for instance, parents do not require from their children a perfect recompense for the gift of life and the many years of generous care and nurturing. Instead, they happily accept the love and respect that can be reasonably expected from children, knowing full well that it is never a strict equality. A similar dynamic is also at work in the worship owed to God in the virtue of religion. Here too, the equality requisite for authentic justice is measured not by a one-to-one equation but in reference to what is reasonably to be expected from the individual. Aquinas argues that this equality of proportion also governs the temporal punishment owed to God for just satisfaction.[24]

The importance of the reference to friendship is not to be overlooked. A man's friendship with God is the essential foundation for the possibility of an equality of proportion. Above all else, this truth reminds us of the fact that

---

[21] *Super Sent.*, lib. 4, dist. 15, q. 1, a. 1, qc. 2: "medium justitiae accipitur secundum adaequationem rei ad rem in proportionalitate aliqua."

[22] *Super Sent.*, lib. 4, dist. 15, q. 1, a. 2.

[23] *Super Sent.*, lib. 4, dist. 15, q. 1, a. 2.

[24] *Super Sent.*, lib. 4, dist. 15, q. 1, a. 2.

the personal satisfaction we offer to God is subordinate to the satisfaction Christ has already offered for us. He has already made reparation for our sins but now calls us to join in that self-offering in a real but limited and subordinate way. It is, therefore, only due to God's gracious acceptance, in view of the relationship of mutual love made possible by Christ, that an equality of strict equivalence is not demanded.[25] It is in light of a man's friendship in charity, in other words, that God accepts an equality of proportion.

Additionally, Aquinas also claims that it is only in virtue of the charity that motivates them that any satisfactory works are acceptable to God at all.[26] Our actions are pleasing to God because they are done out of love for God. Thus, friendship with God in charity is necessary both in order to establish the possibility of a restoration of justice through an equality of proportion and to empower man with the appropriate means. This argument then implicitly underscores the claim made throughout this book that the resolution of man's personal debt of punishment is best understood not before the forgiveness of sin but *after*. It is only after friendship with God has been restored through the forgiveness of sins that the genuine possibility of personal satisfaction is conceivable.

While such a clarification does little to help us quantify the amount of temporal punishment with any precision, it does allow us to consider it in its proper context. The equality of justice that man strives for in works of satisfaction is not based on an exact equivalence. Rather, it is rooted in a relationship of love—it is the justice of friends. At the same time, to say this is not to deny the authenticity of the justice and the reality of the obligation. True charity should fill man with a genuine zeal for making satisfaction to divine justice. Although a man knows that he cannot render an exact equivalent to God, he should strive to do what is possible, as the equality of proportion demands. This equality will vary for each individual according to his state in life[27] and the gravity of sins committed, but it remains, nonetheless, a true equality and a genuine measure for the restoration of justice.

It also follows from what has been said that the quality and intensity of the friendship in some way determines the amount of satisfaction to be demanded. In the confessional, the strength of the friendship is evidenced by the charity of the penitent now manifest in contrition. Aquinas, therefore, argues, "it happens for charity to be so intense in the act that contrition following from it will merit not only the removal of guilt, but also the absolution

---

[25] *Super Sent.*, lib. 4, dist. 15, q. 1, a. 3, qc. 2.

[26] *Super Sent.*, lib. 4, dist. 15, q. 1, a. 3, qc. 2–3.

[27] *Super Sent.*, lib. 4, dist. 15, q. 1, a. 2, ad 3.

from all punishment."[28] The love of the penitent, in other words, can be so profound that God no longer requires any other work to satisfy the demands of divine justice. Greater contrition is a sign of greater friendship with God. Greater friendship with God means a closer union with Christ, and a closer union with Christ means a greater sharing in his goods, one of which is the satisfaction he won for mankind on Calvary. However, even when the penitent does not manifest such a profound and perfect sorrow for sin, the quality of contrition ought to be evaluated in the assessment of a fitting penance.

Additionally, it is also important to take note of the ways in which some of the temporal punishment may have already been satisfied. In particular, the preceding acts of contrition and confession can do much to begin the process of satisfaction. In regard to contrition, Aquinas explains that "the sensible sorrow that the will excites in contrition . . . is also a kind of punishment."[29] Contrition, then, not only plays an important role in determining the amount of temporal punishment to be imposed, as we just saw, but is also an important means of satisfying that debt, even before the sacrament is completed. In a similar way, Aquinas observes that the shame involved in the act of confessing to another human being is penal in nature.[30] It can, therefore, also serve as a kind of anticipatory satisfaction. It follows from these considerations that those who show great sorrow in their contrition and profound humility in their confession can reasonably be given a lighter penance. In important ways, they have already begun to make satisfaction for sin. Finally, Aquinas also argues that the sacramental absolution itself remits some of the temporal punishment.[31] Thus, by the actions of the penitent and through the sacramental power of the priest, a portion of the work of satisfaction is accomplished before the penitent ever leaves the confessional.

Despite this affirmation, in the vast majority of cases, it is safe to assume that some debt of punishment remains to be satisfied, and, as I have said, this is one of the principal reasons why the priest imposes a penance. As Christ's minister, it is, after all, the duty of the confessor to bind the penitent to certain works in view of the satisfaction of divine justice.[32] Through these

---

[28] *Super Sent.*, lib. 4, dist. 17, q. 2, a. 5, qc. 2: "sic contingit tantum intendi caritatem in actu, quod contritio inde sequens merebitur non solum culpae amotionem, sed etiam absolutionem ab omni poena."

[29] *Super Sent.*, lib. 4, dist. 17, q. 2, a. 5, qc. 2: "doloris sensibilis quem voluntas in contritione excitat . . . poena etiam quaedam est"

[30] *ST* IIIa, q. 68, a. 6: "ipsa particularis confessio homini facta est poenosa, propter verecundiam confitentis."

[31] *SCG* IV, cap. 72; *Super Sent.*, lib. 4, dist. 18, q. 1, a. 3, qc. 2, ad 3.

[32] *SCG* IV, cap. 72.

works the reconciled sinner begins to heal his relationship with God and works toward the restoration of justice.[33]

From what has been said until now, the kind of actions to be imposed as a penance should be clear. First and foremost, they must be satisfactory and, therefore, punitive in nature. They must contrast in some way with the will of man. However, as we saw in chapter four, this contrast may be directed against the actual, habitual, or natural will of man. In practice, the works of satisfaction are traditionally divided by the categories of prayer, fasting, and almsgiving. As Aquinas explains:

> Satisfaction, as was said, must be such that something is taken away from us for the honor of God. Now we only have three goods: namely, the soul's goods, the body's goods, and fortune's goods, namely, external goods. We do indeed take something away from ourselves of fortune's goods by almsgiving, and from bodily goods by fasting. But from the soul's goods it is not necessary that we take something away as to their essence or as to their diminishment, for by them we are made acceptable to God; but by the fact that we submit them to God completely, and this happens through prayer.[34]

This categorization is present in many places in the tradition, but it need not be applied too rigorously. As Aquinas explains, the divisions admit of a wide extension. He writes, "Whatever belongs to bodily affliction comes

---

[33] In a couple of texts Aquinas seems to hold that the satisfactory works imposed by the priest in the sacrament of penance *entirely* determine the remaining debt of punishment, at least for the sins that were confessed. In *SCG* IV, cap. 72, he writes concerning the penance assigned by the priest, "Hereby man is wholly freed from the debt of punishment, since he has paid the penalty which he deserved." "Per quam homo totaliter a reatu poenae liberatur, dum poenam exsolvit quam debuit." The "totaliter" of this phrase is significant. See also *Super Sent.*, lib. 4, dist. 17, q. 3, a. 1, qc. 1, ad 4.

However, in light of the great historical variation in penances, it seems more reasonable to presume in today's context that the penance assigned is only a minimal, representational proportion of the total debt of punishment owed to divine justice, thus necessitating ongoing satisfactory works. Nevertheless, even from Aquinas's perspective, some other satisfaction would still be necessary in order to atone for venial sins not brought to the sacramental forum.

[34] *Super Sent.*, lib. 4, dist. 15, q. 1, a. 4, qc. 3: "satisfactio, ut dictum est, debet esse talis per quam aliquid nobis subtrahamus ad honorem Dei. Nos autem non habemus nisi tria bona; scilicet bona animae, bona corporis, et bona fortunae, scilicet exteriora. Ex bonis quidem fortunae subtrahimus aliquid nobis per eleemosynam; sed ex bonis corporalibus per jejunium; ex bonis autem animae non oportet quod aliquid subtrahamus nobis quantum ad essentiam vel quantum ad diminutionem ipsorum, quia per ea efficimur Deo accepti sed per hoc quod ea submittamus Deo totaliter; et hoc fit per orationem."

under the heading of fasting; and whatever is spent on the benefit of one's neighbor has the nature of almsgiving. And likewise, whatever shows worship to God takes the nature of prayer. And so one single work can hold several notions of making satisfaction."[35] Any work, therefore, that can reasonably be fit into one of these categories may be appropriately assigned as a penance and is an adequate means for satisfying divine justice.

EXTRA-SACRAMENTAL SATISFACTION

Even outside of the sacrament of penance, however, the work of satisfaction ought to continue. The very existence of purgatory is evidence of the fact that the debt of temporal punishment often remains even after death. This extra-sacramental form of satisfaction, however, should be referred to the sacramental form as its paradigmatic model. All of the principles that we saw in that context will be relevant here as well and will help to shape the practice of satisfaction throughout one's lifetime.

Of primary importance is the fact that man cannot make satisfaction for sins that have not already been forgiven. As we have seen, the actual reorientation of the will to God is the essential beginning of all the other means of repairing the damage of sin. Justice simply cannot be restored without this foundation. As Aquinas explains, "no one can have his punishment forgiven unless his fault is already forgiven."[36] It follows, therefore, that even outside the confessional, man should first strive with the help of grace to cultivate a profound sense of contrition before concerning himself with the debt of temporal punishment. If the contrition is genuine, it will then prompt man to make the appropriate satisfaction.

Additionally, it is also important to remember the relationship between charity and satisfaction. As we saw, charity is the essential foundation for all satisfactory works. In the first place, it makes satisfactory works possible, and it is also the charity with which these actions are performed that makes them acceptable to God. Thus, although there is reason to take temporal punishment and the debt owed to divine justice seriously, it would be a grave distortion to focus exclusively or even predominantly on this aspect of the spiritual life. The value of charity and the supernatural life far exceeds that

---

[35] *Super Sent.*, lib. 4, dist. 15, q. 1, a. 4, qc. 3, ad 5: "quidquid ad afflictionem corporis pertinet, totum ad jejunium refertur; et quidquid ad proximi utilitatem expenditur, totum elemosynae rationem habet; et similiter quaecumque latria exhibeatur Deo, orationis accipit rationem; et ideo etiam unum opus potest habere plures rationes satisfaciendi."

[36] *Super Sent.*, lib. 4, dist. 20, q. 1, a. 5, qc. 1: "nulli potest dimitti poena, nisi cui jam dimissa est culpa."

of the order of justice. Thus charity, like the contrition included within it, must always be the primary goal.

At the same time, as I have been arguing, true charity and contrition always necessarily include an earnest commitment to making reparation to divine justice by means of satisfactory works throughout one's life. The two dimensions, though distinct, are never *separate*. Charity that does not take note of and attend to the demands of divine justice is not true charity. If a man loves God, then he cannot ignore the equality of divine justice. Even if charity is not reduced to that concern, it cannot neglect it. True charity always leads to satisfaction. That being said, we should also recall that the satisfactory works performed during one's lifetime also lead to a growth in charity. Precisely because they are motivated by charity, in other words, satisfactory works merit an increase in that charity. Those who are intent on making satisfaction for the right reasons often reach the most profound heights of holiness.

We can, therefore, discern a kind of mutual enrichment between charity and satisfaction. Charity prompts man to consider the demands of divine justice and moves him to make fitting reparation through satisfactory works. Those satisfactory works then merit an increase in charity, which then renders man all the more attentive to divine justice, and so the cycle continues.[37]

In the lives of the saints, this dynamic exchange between charity and satisfaction has led to profound and heroic acts of love and reparation. The examples are as varied as are the saints themselves, but the supreme expression of this movement is the voluntary submission to death in martyrdom. In the words of our Lord, "Greater love has no man than this, that a man lay down his life for his friends."[38] By dying for God in this way, the martyr perfectly conforms himself to Christ, who gave up his life for us in the supreme sacrifice of love. In this sense, the martyr, like Christ, makes perfect, superabundant satisfaction for his sins. Aquinas even argues that this radical conformity to Christ in martyrdom is comparable to that of baptism. It brings with it "the full deliverance from guilt and punishment."[39] It is certain, then, that upon his death, the martyr enters immediately into the joy of heaven.

---

[37] It should also be noted that, at times, performing satisfactory or penitential works can be a helpful psychological aid in taking the life of charity and grace seriously. The mutual enrichment of satisfaction and charity thus comes from multiple angles.

[38] John 15:13.

[39] *ST* IIIa, q. 68, a. 2, ad 2: "plenam liberationem a culpa et poena."

Conclusion

Although the prospect of temporal punishment and divine retributive justice appears sobering, the account I have presented in this chapter has shown the place of satisfaction in God's healing work during this life. The work of perfect satisfaction for every human sin has been accomplished by Christ in virtue of the great love by which the God-man laid down his life. Nevertheless, when man sins after baptism he is invited through the grace of Christ and the sacrament of penance to cooperate in his own healing by taking a share in the work of satisfaction.

Such satisfaction, however, does not demand a strict "equality of quantity," which only Christ himself could offer, but is rather based on an "equality of proportion." According to this measure, God demands from the soul that which is possible and reasonable according to his state in life, his condition, and the relative gravity of his sins, considering at the same time the intensity of his friendship with him.

Moved, then, by the love of God and repentance for his sins, man responds with prayer, fasting, and almsgiving in order to do his part in restoring the equality of divine justice. If this work is accomplished at the end of man's life, he enters immediately into heaven where he justly spends eternity with the God whom he loves above all else. If not, as we have seen in the preceding chapters, he is purified of any remaining debt of punishment in purgatory.

From this perspective, the centrality of charity comes to the fore yet again. Even in our appropriate concern for making reparation to divine justice, it must be charity that guides all of our actions. It is, after all, only the love of God that makes personal satisfaction possible.

CHAPTER VI

The Exchange of Satisfaction and the Theology of Indulgences

IN THE PREVIOUS CHAPTER we have seen the place of personal satisfaction in man's life and the means to undertake that responsibility. In particular, I emphasized the essential relationship between charity and satisfaction. As we saw, the dynamic exchange between these two realities led the saints to great heights of self-denial, the greatest example of which is martyrdom. In that great act many saints have radically conformed themselves to Christ and have offered more than sufficient satisfaction for all of their sins.

In additional to personal satisfaction, however, it is also possible for Christians to offer satisfaction for one another. Christ our head has already shown us the way. He, after all, did just that when he bore the weight of our sins on Calvary. Offering satisfaction for others thus brings a further kind of conformity to Christ than that of simply cooperating in our own healing by personal satisfaction. To put it simply, union with Christ is deepened by making satisfaction for our brothers and sisters just as Christ did. This possibility, however, is in need of explanation, and the first part of this chapter will be dedicated to this task.

As we will then see, the ability to make satisfaction for another is also the foundation of the Church's practice of indulgences. Beyond even our personal satisfactory works, these gifts of the Church provide the most significant means of remitting temporal punishment while on earth. For reasons we will see, our own efforts pale in comparison to the satisfaction available to man by means of indulgences. Because of the technical precision required, the theology of indulgences will occupy the bulk of this chapter. Nevertheless, as we will see, the theology of indulgences follows all of the principles laid out for the interpersonal sharing of satisfaction. The only difference is that in the case of indulgences, the authority of the Church intervenes to wisely direct the effects of satisfaction for the benefit of her members.

SHARING THE WORK OF SATISFACTION

In the course of her history, the superabundant satisfaction of the martyrs helped to lead the Church gradually to a more conscious recognition of the possibility of making satisfaction for others. In the early Church, penitents sought the intercession of those destined for martyrdom in order to reduce their own portion of temporal punishment.[1] Because of the eminent charity of these saints and the excess of satisfaction offered to God through their impending death, in certain circumstances it seemed reasonable to abbreviate the penance required of other Christians. At the beginning of the Decian persecution in Africa, for example, St. Cyprian claimed the intercession of these "confessors" as a justification for reconciling sinners who were seriously ill before they had completed their assigned penance.[2]

Implicit in this reasoning, as I suggested, is a recognition of the fact that it is possible for one Christian to make satisfaction for another. This idea is particularly evident in the case of the martyrs, but the same dynamic also applies to any form of legitimate satisfaction. The sharing of satisfactory works is possible because of the kind of justice involved. In the previous chapter, I argued that the justice of personal satisfaction is based on an equality of proportion. In saying this, I showed that the relationship between the sinner and God is of primary importance in determining the quantity of punishment, that is, the specific proportion to be applied in a particular case. However, this distinction should not lead us to think of the debt of punishment exclusively in terms of an exchange between individuals. Rather, punitive justice, as we saw in chapter three, primarily concerns the social order itself. In the case of sin, it is the universal moral order, with God as its head and principle, that has been offended. Therefore, although ordinarily it is the guilty one himself who bears the burden of restoring the order of justice through the endurance of a fitting punishment, others may, under certain conditions, voluntarily and mercifully decide to share in the sinner's burden. To do so is to make satisfaction for another. This principle serves as the foundation of both Christ's satisfaction for us and of our offering satisfaction for our brothers and sisters.

Here again, however, the union of charity is of foundational importance. Just as one cannot make satisfaction for himself without the charity that renders his works acceptable to God, neither can anyone make satisfaction for another without being united to him in charity. Charity is what unites

---

[1] Bernhard Poschmann, *Penance and Anointing of the Sick*, trans. Francis Courtney (Eugene, OR: Wipf and Stock, 1964), 76.

[2] Poschmann, *Penance and Anointing of the Sick*, 77.

them in the communion of saints, and beyond simply belonging to the same moral order of divine justice, the exchange of satisfaction requires this supernatural bond.[3] To put it simply, it is only insofar as the two become "one in Christ Jesus" that the satisfaction of one can ease the debt of the other.[4]

Nevertheless, the union of the two does not mean that the satisfactory work simply benefits both of them. If one man offers his satisfaction for another, the remission of temporal punishment truly passes to the other. As Aquinas explains, "someone who makes satisfaction for another does not make satisfaction for himself, for that amount of punishment does not suffice for both sins."[5] Unlike grace and charity, which are common goods and are, therefore, not reduced when divided and shared, satisfaction only has a limited value.[6] Thus, when a satisfactory work is offered entirely for the benefit of another, the one performing the work does not lessen his own debt of punishment.[7] At the same time, Aquinas is quick to note that this work does benefit the one who performs it by meriting eternal life for him.[8] This grace, he explains, is far greater than a mere remission of temporal punishment. It is, therefore, an admirable practice to voluntarily offer satisfactory works for others. It is a way that we can "bear one another's burdens," as St. Paul recommends.[9] In doing so, we both lighten the suffering of a fellow Christian and grow personally in grace and charity at the same time.

Because of the divisibility of satisfaction just identified, it is necessary that man form an explicit intention in order to offer his satisfaction for another. The good of satisfaction must be directed.[10] When "offering up" one's penances, therefore, it is a good practice to have a specific beneficiary in mind.

It is also possible, however, simply to offer one's satisfaction generically. This was done, in fact, by many of the great saints. According to Aquinas, these heroic Christians performed their works of satisfaction not for a specific individual but for the good of the whole Christian community. He writes:

---

3   *Super Sent.*, lib. 4, dist. 45, q. 2, a. 1, qc. 2.

4   Gal 3:28. It should go without saying that the one for whom a man offers satisfaction must also be in a state of grace.

5   *Super Sent.*, lib. 4, dist. 20, q. 1, a. 2, qc. 3, ad 3: "non autem qui pro alio satisfacit, pro se satisfacit; quia illa quantitas poenae non sufficit ad utrumque peccatum."

6   *Super Sent.*, lib. 4, dist. 45, q. 2, a. 4, qc. 2.

7   In *Super Sent.*, lib. 4, dist. 20, q. 1, a. 2, qc. 3 Aquinas remarks that the charity that motivates a man to offer his satisfaction for another means that less satisfaction is required in this case than if the sinner offered satisfaction for himself.

8   *Super Sent.*, lib. 4, dist. 20, q. 1, a. 2, qc. 3, ad 3.

9   Gal 6:2.

10   Cf. *Super Sent.*, lib. 4, dist. 45, q. 2, a. 1, qc. 2.

Now, the saints, in whom this superabundance of satisfactory works is found, did not do works like this specifically for the person who needs forgiveness, otherwise he would have obtained forgiveness without any indulgence. But they did it for the Church as a whole, as the Apostle says: he *will fill up in his own body what is lacking from Christ's Passion for the sake of the church.*[11]

According to Aquinas, because the generic, superabundant satisfaction of the saints was not offered for particular individuals, it became the common possession of the whole Church.[12] Traditionally, this common possession is referred to as the "treasury of the satisfaction of Christ and the saints."[13] Beyond mere interpersonal sharing, then, this treasury serves as the foundation for the Church's practice of indulgences. By dispensing of this treasury, the Church offers the faithful an invaluable resource for the remission of temporal punishment.

INDULGENCES

As we have just seen, the saints, in union with Christ, have entrusted to the Church a great treasury of satisfaction. Through their heroic charity and voluntary self-renunciation, often to the point of death, they have done more than enough to satisfy for their own sins and have left the Church a great and abundant surplus. In virtue of her governing mission, it is the prerogative of the Church to apply that excess of satisfaction to those whom she sees fit. As Aquinas explains, "those things that are shared by any multitude are distributed to the multitude individually according to the decision of whoever is in charge of the multitude."[14] When the Church authoritatively distributes this treasury of satisfaction to the faithful, it is called an indulgence.[15]

---

[11] *Super Sent.*, lib. 4, dist. 20, q. 1, a. 3, qc. 1: "Sancti autem in quibus superabundantia operum satisfactionis invenitur, non determinate pro isto qui remissione indiget, hujusmodi opera fecerunt: alias absque omni indulgentia remissionem consequeretur: sed communiter pro tota Ecclesia, sicut apostolus dicit se implere ea quae desunt passioni Christi in corpore suo pro Ecclesia."

[12] *Super Sent.*, lib. 4, dist. 20, q. 1, a. 3, qc. 1.

[13] CCC, §1471; Paul VI, *Indulgentiarum Doctrina*, norm 1.

[14] *Super Sent.*, lib. 4, dist. 20, q. 1, a. 3, qc 1: "Ea autem quae sunt communia multitudinis alicujus, distribuuntur singulis de multitudine secundum arbitrium ejus qui multitudini praeest."

[15] Indulgences can hardly be mentioned today without calling to mind the controversy with Luther in the sixteenth century. For an interesting analysis of the relationship between the soteriology of Luther and the Catholic theology of indulgences, see Mary C. Moorman, *Indulgences: Luther, Catholicism, and the Imputation of Merit* (Steubenville, OH: Emmaus Academic, 2017).

In this line, it is important to note that an indulgence is not an outright forgiveness or dismissal of temporal punishment due to God, but a genuine payment. In other words, an indulgence is not a substitute for satisfaction but serves as an alternative means toward that end. The debt is not overlooked or forgotten but is paid on behalf of the sinner from the treasury of the Church. As Aquinas explains, "Someone who receives indulgences is not absolved, simply speaking, from the debt of punishment; but he is given what will pay the debt."[16] Only God himself can forgive the debt outright. The Church, for her part, has an abundant treasury and can use it on behalf of her members.

That being said, the Church is not free simply to dispense the satisfaction at whim. Rather, as with any gift, she must respect the intention of the giver. In the case of the ecclesiastical treasury, the saints performed their works for the honor of God and the benefit of the Church. The Church, therefore, can only give indulgences to the faithful on the condition that those who receive them also perform a work for the honor of God and the benefit of the Church.[17] In this way, the intention of the saints is fully respected. Accordingly, the Church *indulgences* certain pious actions when she adds a gift of additional satisfaction to them. When the faithful perform these works, they receive from the treasury of the Church a greater remission of temporal punishment than the works themselves would ordinarily have merited.

It should be noted, however, that, according to Aquinas, the just cause for the granting of an indulgence does not necessarily need to be proportionate.[18] There need be no balance or equality between the objective value of the action performed and the benefit that the Church associates with it. The very logic of indulgences suggests that the gift is, at least potentially, in excess of the value of the work performed. Although some action is required of the faithful in order to receive an indulgence, the efficacy comes from the authoritative application of the Church's treasury to the individual. An indulgence is not, therefore, a just reward but, rather, a gratuitous gift. All that matters is that the gift be given to someone for the same reasons that the saints entrusted it to the Church in the first place: the glory of God and the benefit of the Church.

It follows from this distinction that the Church has a limited but real freedom in its distribution and organization of indulgences. As is wise and prudent, the Church uses this privilege for the benefit of her children by

---

[16] *Super Sent.*, lib. 4, dist. 20, q. 1, a. 3, qc. 1, ad 2: "iste qui indulgentias suscipit, non absolvitur, simpliciter loquendo, a debito poenae; sed datur sibi unde debitum solvat."

[17] *Super Sent.*, lib. 4, dist. 20, q. 1, a. 3, qc. 2

[18] *Super Sent.*, lib. 4, dist. 20, q. 1, a. 3, qc. 2.

indulgencing those actions which she judges most beneficial for them. It is a kind of spiritual incentive, to put it simply. By associating a gift of the remission of temporal punishment with certain works, the Church encourages the faithful to perform the actions that are most salutary for their spiritual lives. Typical examples of this include visiting the Blessed Sacrament, reading the Scriptures, and praying the Rosary.

In this way, the Church also respects the distinction highlighted repeatedly throughout this book concerning charity and satisfaction. While the satisfactory element of an action remits temporal punishment, the fact that it is done with charity merits an increase of grace, and this latter reward is of far greater value. Aquinas explains that the merit of eternal rewards is "infinitely better than the dismissal of temporal punishment."[19] Temporal punishment, after all, though serious, is not a matter of salvation.[20] The Church's primary motivation in the dispensation of indulgences, therefore, is to incite her children to grow in grace and charity through the performance of holy works. Importantly, but only secondarily, she also wants to help them reduce their debt of punishment before divine justice.

This consideration also answers the question of those who ask why the Church, if she has this authority, does not simply immediately remit the temporal punishment of all the faithful throughout the world. Why not pour forth the treasury all at once? In light of what has been said, it is clear that to do so would undermine her primary motivation. The remission of temporal punishment would be of little value if the faithful were not challenged to grow in charity in the process. The practice of the Church imitates that of God who, as we have seen, often allows us to endure the consequences and penalties of sin during this life so that we might turn to him with greater faith, hope, and charity.

Ecclesiastical Law

It, therefore, falls within authority of the Church to set the parameters for the granting of indulgences. In particular, she must determine the "amount" of remission to grant for each work, the generic conditions for the granting of an indulgence, and the specific actions that will be indulgenced, among other things. Because these are free decisions of the Church, the particular

---

[19] *Super Sent.*, lib. 4, dist. 20, q. 1, a. 3, qc. 2, ad 2: "in infinitum melius est quam dimissio poenae temporalis."

[20] At the same time, as I have said, to completely neglect this aspect of divine justice is incompatible with an authentic love of God.

determinations form a part of ecclesiastical law. Specifically, the current legislation governing indulgences is contained in the *Manual of Indulgences: Norms and Grants (Enchiridion Indulgentiarum: Normae et Concessiones)*, promulgated by the Apostolic Penitentiary in 1999.[21]

According to these norms of the Church and her traditional practice, indulgences are first distinguished by their partial or plenary nature. Plenary indulgences remit all of the temporal punishment due to sin, and partial indulgences only a part.

The Church has taken different approaches to the distribution of partial indulgences in her history. Many Catholics have come across old prayer books or holy cards that include a reference to an indulgence worth a certain number of days or years. At one time, for example, making the sign of the cross with holy water received an indulgence of one hundred days.[22] As should be clear, however, this assignment of time did not correspond to "days" or "years" in purgatory. The time of the separated soul, as we have seen, is discontinuous and is not measured by solar time. Rather, the "time" associated with an indulgence referred to the amount of temporal punishment that would have been remitted by undertaking that amount of penance according to the prior norms of canonical penance.[23] A one hundred days' indulgence, for example, conferred on the one who received it a remission of as much temporal punishment as would have been remitted if the person had performed the prescribed penance of the Church for one hundred days. Needless to say, the generosity of the Church in these concessions was extraordinary.

The logic of this measurement is rooted in the very history of the practice of indulgences. As we have seen, there is an intentional relationship between the punishment owed before God and the practices of satisfaction imposed by the Church. By requiring certain penances, the Church strives to be a kind of sacrament of divine justice in such a way that she incarnates the demands of divine justice in the lives of the faithful. The penance to be performed on earth is always to be considered, therefore, in reference to the debt of punishment owed to God. The relationship between the two, even if imperfect, must always be kept in mind. In this sense, there is an inherent intelligibility in measuring the remission of the divine penalty by means of its temporal corollary.

---

[21] Apostolic Penitentiary, *Manual of Indulgences: Norms and Grants* (Washington, DC: USCCB, 1999).

[22] Charles J. Callan, O.P., and John A. McHugh, *Blessed Be God: A Complete Catholic Prayer Book* (Boonville, NY: Preserving Christian Publications, 2016), 1.

[23] Ludwig Ott, *Fundamentals of Catholic Dogma*, trans. Patrick Lynch, ed. James Canon Bastible (Charlotte, NC: Tan Books, 1974), 443.

This instinct may have been more intuitive in the early history of the Church when the penances were more intense and must have been seen to bear a more direct connection to the debt owed to divine justice. Today the satisfaction imposed by the minister in the sacrament of penance (although proportionate and appropriate) is often merely a minimal representational proportion of the total satisfaction owed to God. One gets the sense, however, that in the early Church there was a greater effort to coordinate the two. Penances were long and difficult and were typically determined by strictly regulated canons.[24] For particularly grave sins, for example, a penance of several years was often imposed.[25] During that time, the penitent might be enrolled in the formal *ordo paenitentium* in the Church to which certain restrictions and obligations were legally attached.[26] These practices could include remaining in the back of the church during the liturgy, exclusion from Communion, the wearing of a penitential garment, special prayers, fasting, sexual abstinence, the curtailment of sleep, and almsgiving, among other things.[27]

Because these penances were imposed by the Church, they were primarily a matter of ecclesiastical jurisdiction. They were subject, in other words, to the regulation of Church authorities. The diocesan bishop, for example, had a certain ability to adapt the regulations to particular circumstances.[28] That being said, the ecclesiastical penance was not a standalone reality. It always bore an intentional connection to the satisfaction owed to God. For this reason, the penance could not be dispensed with arbitrarily without the risk of neglecting divine justice. To fail to impose a just penance would have been considered gravely irresponsible.

In various stages, the distinction between the two requirements (the formally imposed ecclesiastical penance and the satisfaction owed to divine justice) and the relative subordination of the ecclesiastical to the divine gradually led to the recognition of the possibility of mitigating the ecclesiastical penance when the Church could ensure that satisfaction was being made to divine justice by another means. When divine justice was satisfied, the ecclesiastical penance lost some of its necessity. As I suggested earlier, this first happened through the intercession of the "confessors" awaiting their martyrdom. By recourse to their heroic self-denial, the Church found warrant for reducing or eliminating the penances of those in desperate

---

[24] Poschmann, *Penance and Anointing of the Sick*, 82. Because of these canons, the early penitential practice of the Church is often referred to as "canonical penance."

[25] Poschmann, *Penance and Anointing of the Sick*, 95.

[26] Poschmann, *Penance and Anointing of the Sick*, 87.

[27] Poschmann, *Penance and Anointing of the Sick*, 88–89.

[28] Poschmann, *Penance and Anointing of the Sick*, 93–94.

circumstances. To put it simply, because these martyrs were making super-abundant satisfaction, it was reasonable to require less ecclesiastical penance of other members of the Church.

In different ways, the medieval Church also had recourse to extra-sacramental means for alleviating the debt of temporal punishment before both God and the Church. The days of the early martyrs had passed, but penitents could still be assisted by the intervention and vicarious satisfaction of other Christians.[29] With regard to ecclesiastical penances, the Church slowly developed a complex system of redemptions by which the faithful could commute their penance for more manageable practices.[30] A particularly arduous penance, for example, could be substituted for a pilgrimage, a shorter but more intense period of fasting, almsgiving, or entering a monastery, among other things.[31] These redemptions did not technically reduce the penance, since they were allowed on the principle that they represented an even exchange. Nevertheless, in practice, they allowed the faithful to complete penances that would otherwise have taken more than a lifetime. As in ancient times, the "tariffed" penances of the Middle Ages followed elaborate regulations that often called for severe and rigorous discipline.

Because the redemptions merely exchanged one penance for another, however, they were not understood to offer any direct reduction of the temporal punishment owed to God. For this purpose, medieval Christians sought out special "absolutions," intercessory prayers performed by the pope or bishop on behalf of the faithful for the remission of their temporal punishment. These prayers were thought to have a particular efficacy because of their authoritative nature.[32] Typically, they were offered to the faithful on special occasions and feasts throughout the year. Even though they did not reduce the ecclesiastical or canonical penance imposed on the faithful, these absolutions were eagerly desired because of the relief that they offered from the punishments to be expected in the life to come.

The indulgence then arose as a combination of the medieval redemption and absolution. Because of the remission of temporal punishment before God obtained by the authoritative intervention of the Church (as with absolutions), the Church could now justify not merely an exchange of penance (as with redemptions) but even a simple reduction. In the coordination of the two components (divine and ecclesial), the theoretical penitential

---

29 Poschmann, *Penance and Anointing of the Sick*, 211.
30 Poschmann, *Penance and Anointing of the Sick*, 127.
31 Poschmann, *Penance and Anointing of the Sick*, 127, 150–52.
32 Poschmann, *Penance and Anointing of the Sick*, 212.

equivalence of the former redemptions was no longer required. Now, in light of the remission of temporal punishment before God, a reduction of the ecclesiastical penance was both possible and reasonable. In the early days of indulgences, in other words, those who gained them received not only a remission of temporal punishment before God but also a reduction of their ecclesiastical penances.[33] The combination of these two elements was, therefore, the initial distinguishing feature of indulgences. By recourse to these special gifts of the Church, an otherwise long and arduous penance could be significantly mitigated without the risk of neglecting divine justice.

In this context, while still maintaining the distinction between the divine and the ecclesiastical aspects, it was natural to refer to the "quantity" of the remission of temporal punishment before God by reference to the amount of ecclesiastical penance being dispensed. An indulgence was, therefore, described in terms of the number of days or years of ecclesiastical penance that it remitted, and the understanding was that an equivalent amount of temporal punishment was also being remitted before God.

At the end of the Middle Ages, however, the practice of canonical and "tariffed" penances slowly declined,[34] and the measurement of indulgences by means of days of penance consequently lost its intuitive value. The measurement by days and years continued to serve as a kind of traditional benchmark or legal fiction for describing the relative value of indulgences, but, without the ecclesial counterpart, the time of an indulgence referred exclusively to the amount of temporal punishment before God that would have been remitted by the performance of that many days of the old canonical penance (now outdated). As I suggested above, for example, a one hundred days indulgence was worth the remission of as much temporal punishment before God as would have been gained from performing one hundred days of the canonical penance, even if the ecclesiastical component was no longer relevant in practice.

Admittedly, despite its value, this system often led to confusion for those unfamiliar with the historical genesis of indulgences. Not a few of the faithful have initially presumed that the time of an indulgence referred directly to time in purgatory. That being said, it is difficult, if not impossible, to conceive of any suitable alternative metric by which to objectively distinguish the relative value of partial indulgences. Without direct access to purgatorial "time," it is impossible to "measure" the amount of purgatory except by comparison with its terrestrial corollary.

---

[33] Poschmann, *Penance and Anointing of the Sick*, 215.

[34] Poschmann, *Penance and Anointing of the Sick*, 153–54.

In order to avoid this difficulty, in recent years the Church has moved to an alternative system for partial indulgences. Instead of distinguishing them from one another by means of varying relative values extrinsically assigned by the Church, partial indulgences are now distinguished by the intrinsic value of the work performed. Today, to be specific, a partial indulgence grants an equal remission of temporal punishment before God as is obtained by the very performance of the indulgenced work itself.[35] To put it simply, those who recite an indulgenced prayer now receive twice the remission of temporal punishment as they would have if the prayer were not indulgenced. Half of the remission comes from their own action, half from the authoritative intervention of the Church on their behalf.

This system removes the distinction of partial indulgences from the adjudication of the Church and places it exclusively on the nature of the action performed and the subjective quality of its performance. Not only does this eliminate the confusion regarding the time of purgatory, but it also has the advantage of providing additional incentive. Because an indulgence is a juridical act, its effect is automatic. When it is applied, in other words, the effect is guaranteed. In practice, this principle means that, under the old system of conferral, a poorly performed indulgence and one performed with great reverence and devotion received the same reward (from the perspective of the authoritative imputation of the treasury of satisfaction of the Church, charity notwithstanding). Performing the action particularly well was not required to receive the indulgence. Under the new system, however, because the subjective quality of the action is directly involved in the measurement of the reward, the faithful are incentivized not only to perform the action but to perform it well. Today, a quick and relatively thoughtless sign of the cross is still indulgenced, but it is not worth nearly as much as one performed piously and devoutly.

Beyond these partial indulgences, there are still many plenary indulgences available. No complex system of measurement, however, is required to make the excellence of this gift intelligible. Those who receive a plenary indulgence have no further debt of punishment before divine justice. It does not matter whether they ought to have suffered a great deal for years of grievous sins or whether they had already offered much satisfaction to God. The plenary indulgence completes the process. With respect to divine punishment, the plenary indulgence, therefore, is just as effective as baptism. Those who perfectly receive a plenary indulgence in their final moment on earth surely go immediately to heaven.

---

[35] *Manual of Indulgences*, Norms on Indulgences, no. 4.

Fortunately, the actions which the Church has designated for this reward, though immensely salutary for the spiritual life, are not particularly difficult. Examples include visiting the Blessed Sacrament for adoration for at least half an hour, devoutly reciting the Rosary in a church or oratory, and reading Sacred Scripture for at least half an hour, among other things.[36] Such concessions are a sign of the Church's great generosity and remind us of her primary motivation: the growth in charity of the faithful.

In addition to the particular action, however, the Church also requires certain additional conditions for obtaining a plenary indulgence: "sacramental confession, Eucharistic communion, and prayer for the intention of the Sovereign Pontiff."[37] The relevant norm states that conditions may be fulfilled several days before or after the performance of the work. Nevertheless, it also notes that it is fitting that communion and prayer for the Holy Father be performed on the same day as the indulgenced action.

In addition, one also often hears that it is necessary to be free from all attachment to sin, even venial sin, in order to gain a plenary indulgence, and the Church states as much in the norm cited above.[38] This requirement does not read as an additional fourth condition, however, but seems to be a clarification about the nature of a plenary indulgence itself. Nevertheless, in light of what I have presented in this book, a question immediately arises. Is the attachment to sin mentioned here a residual evil disposition, or is it a will still actually disordered (guilty) in some way?

The question is one of no little import. If the attachment to be excluded is simply guilt, then, although difficult, the attainment of the goal seems possible. Certainly, it is challenging to offer such perfect and thorough contrition that one's will is truly and entirely reordered to God. However, in moments of deep devotion, such fervor is possible, even if certain evil dispositions still remain. If, however, the attachment to be excluded is any evil disposition, the goal is much more difficult. Evil dispositions, as we have seen, are not usually entirely rectified by a single moment of fervor. Outside of an extraordinary grace, the complete elimination of evil dispositions is almost impossible. There is typically little hope of this goal for the sinner who has spent his life steeped in sin. To be sure, he can rid himself of guilt and be filled with the grace of God. He can begin, even in an instant, to live a profound life of grace—his former ways need not hold him back from the life of God. Nevertheless, he often remains plagued and tempted by the

---

[36] *Manual of Indulgences*, Other Concessions, introduction, 4.

[37] *Manual of Indulgences*, Norms on Indulgences, no. 20, §1.

[38] *Manual of Indulgences*, Norms on Indulgences, no. 20, §1.

habits he spent years forming. Thus, if the affection that impedes a plenary indulgence is an evil disposition, the number of those who can hope to receive one is significantly limited.

We have already seen, however, the theological resources to solve the dilemma. As I have argued, there is no immediate connection between evil dispositions and the debt of punishment before God. They do both result from sinful actions, but they are not strictly dependent on one another. Thus, there is no necessary reason why the remission of temporal punishment would require freedom from all evil dispositions. In contrast, the remission of temporal punishment does require the restoration of friendship with God and the forgiveness of guilt. One cannot, as we saw, make satisfaction for a sin that has not already been forgiven. Furthermore, if forgiveness is required to make personal satisfaction, it is also required to receive the vicarious satisfaction of others. Consequently, freedom from all guilt is a necessary condition for receiving a plenary indulgence precisely because the latter includes the remission of all temporal punishment. If a man retains even the slightest venial sin, he simply cannot have *all* of his temporal punishment remitted.[39]

In line with this interpretation, it is better to regard the affection that impedes a plenary indulgence as the logical contrary to the true contrition which repents of past wrong deeds. Contrition, as we have seen, even when only virtually included in a fervent act of charity, is a necessary part of the forgiveness of sin. Attachment to sin—an unwillingness to renounce some prior sin—is, in contrast, directly opposed to this movement of love.[40] One cannot receive forgiveness for a sin, in other words, if one's will still clings to it, even if only in a subtle and hidden way. To be truly free to receive the benefit of a plenary indulgence, one must be willing to repent of each and every sin out of a complete love of God.

It is, therefore, a lingering guilt that this condition ultimately excludes, rather than an evil disposition. The Church's caution here thus echoes

---

[39] This understanding has been the interpretation of many in the Church's theological tradition. The Bouscaren and Ellis commentary on the 1917 Code of Canon Law, for example, explains that, "it is impossible for a person to gain for himself an indulgence which is absolutely plenary in its effect, as long as he remains guilty of any slightest venial sin." T. Lincoln Bouscaren, S.J., and Adam C. Ellis, S.J., *Canon Law: A Text and Commentary* (Milwaukee, WI: The Bruce Publishing Company, 1948), 336. The commentary then cites the authority of Vermeersch and St. Alphonsus in support of the position that when any guilt of venial sin does remain, the plenary indulgence remits all temporal punishment except for that which is due for the venial sin whose guilt is not yet forgiven (336).

[40] Edward McIlmail, "Indulgence Clarification: Total Detachment from Sin," November 18, 2010, accessed July 17, 2020, https://spiritualdirection.com/2010/11/18/what-is-total-detachment-from-sin-more-indulgence-clarification.

the theological truth that one cannot receive the remission of temporal punishment for a sin that has not been forgiven. Certainly, this principle does not deny that some disposition toward sin may still linger in the will. Nevertheless, as we have seen, to be disposed toward sin is not the same as being unwilling to renounce it. If one truly repents of all past sins out of a love for God and is determined never to sin again, then in the moment that he performs the indulgenced action he will gain the grace of a plenary indulgence. However, any attachment to sin—any unwillingness to abandon past or future sin—negates this possibility. If, therefore, it is necessary to perform partially indulgenced actions with devotion and fervor, we now see that this is all the more true with plenary indulgences. We must let the love of God direct all our actions with fervor and devotion if we hope to receive these gifts as the Church intends.

Indulgences Offered for the Dead

The idea of offering personal satisfaction for the dead presents no great difficulty in light of the possibility of vicarious satisfaction outlined above. The same bond of charity that exists between living Christians also extends to those who have died. This bond of charity, as I explained above, is what makes the sharing of satisfaction possible. Certainly, then, it is possible to offer personal satisfactory works for the souls in purgatory in order to alleviate their suffering and shorten their time in purgatory.

As the logic of this chapter would further suggest, in addition to personal works it is also possible to offer indulgences for the dead. Nevertheless, the juridical nature of an indulgence means that this possibility requires a distinct justification. In the case of personal satisfactory works, considered in abstraction from any indulgence that may be associated with them, the person performing the work is free to direct the satisfaction to whomever he desires, so long as the bond of charity unites them. Because it is his action, he is free to offer it for another. An indulgence, however, though granted in response to an action performed, is a gift of the Church. It is something received, rather than a work performed. For this reason, its application is determined by the conditions of the one bestowing the gift. Consequently, it is not within the power of the recipient to "redirect" the intention of the Church unless he is explicitly given this permission.

In Aquinas's day, some indulgences permitted application to the dead and others did not.[41] Today, however, the Church universally grants this

---

[41] *Super Sent.*, lib. 4, dist. 45, q. 2, a. 3, qc. 2.

permission for every indulgence. The third norm of the current *Manual of Indulgences* states, "The faithful can obtain partial or plenary indulgences for themselves, or they can apply them to the dead by way of suffrage."[42] It is always possible, therefore, to offer an indulgence received for the benefit of a soul in purgatory.

At the same time, it is important to remember the principles of Aquinas outlined above concerning the sharing of satisfaction. With regard to satisfaction, what is offered for another is not retained by the one offering it. In other words, the one who generously offers an indulgence for a soul in purgatory does not personally receive the benefits of the indulgence. His own temporal punishment is not remitted. However, as we also saw above, by this gracious act he does grow in charity. It is an extremely generous and charitable thing to have such concern for one's brothers and sisters in need. As we have seen repeatedly, the charity of the action and the growth in grace that comes from it are of much greater value than the remission of temporal punishment granted by the indulgence.

The phrasing of the norm that gives the permission to offer indulgences for the dead contains technical language and is in need of clarification. "By way of suffrage" or *per modum suffragii* is meant to distinguish the means of offering an indulgence for the dead from the way that an indulgence is obtained for oneself. When the Church confers an indulgence on the person performing the work, she does so "by way of absolution" or *per modum absolutionis*. "Absolution" here refers not to the forgiveness of sin but to the authoritative payment of the debt of punishment out of the Church's treasury of satisfaction.[43] When an indulgence is "redirected" to one of the faithful departed, however, it is said to be offered "by way of suffrage" or *per modum suffragii*. It is offered to God, in other words, for the soul in purgatory as a kind of intercessory suffrage.

The precise wording of this distinction was formulated in the decree *Cum postquam*, written by Pope Leo X to the renowned baroque Thomist and papal legate Cajetan de Vio,[44] but the foundational principle is already present in Aquinas's writing. Indulgences, Aquinas explains, only directly benefit the living because only they are capable of performing the works necessary for gaining an indulgence. They are only transferred to the dead

---

[42] *Manual of Indulgences*, Norms on Indulgences, no. 3.

[43] Charles Journet, "Teologia delle Indulgenze" (Italian version of the original French article cited in the introduction) (1966), 19, accessed July 2020, https://it.scribd.com/document/33798703/Ch-Journet-Teologia-delle-indulgenze.

[44] Denzinger, *Compendium*, §§1447–1449.

"secondarily and indirectly."[45] Similarly important is the fact that the Church only has jurisdiction over the souls on earth and thus can only authoritatively apply the surplus of satisfaction to them.[46] For these two reasons, she is certainly free to transfer the benefit of an indulgence to the dead but can only do so indirectly and by means of suffrage or intercession.[47]

There are at least two implications that follow from this distinction between offering an indulgence *per modum absolutionis* and *per modum suffragii*. First, because an indulgence offered for the dead must initially be received by a living Christian and only secondarily "redirected," the person performing the indulgenced work must be in a state of grace.[48] If the Church were simply applying the indulgence directly to the soul in purgatory, this condition would not be necessary. Hypothetically, in this case, the Church could apply the indulgence on behalf of the deceased on the condition that one of the living performs a certain work without requiring that said person be informed by charity. However, because the "redirection" intentionally passes through the living Christian, that person must be in a state of grace. Without the bond of charity, the person receiving the indulgence cannot worthily offer anything to God. Thus, it is not possible for souls living outside of God's love to offer the benefit of an indulgence for their loved ones in purgatory. We see, therefore, another reason why it is so important to remain always united to God in charity.

Second, because the indulgence passes to those who reside outside of the realm of the Church's direct authority, she cannot guarantee its effect in the same authoritative way.[49] There is reason to hope that God accepts the offering, but the exact measure of its benefit remains a mystery. One cannot be sure, to put it simply, that a plenary indulgence will always immediately free a soul in purgatory. Certainly, it will do him much good, but the ultimate effectiveness is completely in God's hands. A helpful analogy could be made to a wealthy man who seeks to pay off the debt of both his son and a friend. The man to whom his son owes some repayment must accept the money from the boy's father, in whose care the boy resides. In the case of the friend, however, the creditor is free to accept the intervention or not. In a similar way, the jurisdiction of the Church gives her the ability to apply the

---

[45] *Super Sent.*, lib. 4, dist. 45, q. 2, a. 3, qc. 2: "Secundario autem et indirecte."

[46] Ott, *Fundamentals*, 443–44.

[47] This doctrine explains the practice of repeatedly offering plenary indulgences for the same deceased soul. Because that indulgence is offered *per modum suffragii*, the effect cannot be certain, even if the living person who first obtains the indulgence perfectly fulfills all the conditions.

[48] Cf. Poschmann, *Penance and Anointing of the Sick*, 229.

[49] Journet, "Teologia delle Indulgenze," 17; Ott, *Fundamentals*, 443–44.

treasury of the satisfaction authoritatively on behalf of the living. They are her subjects. In the case of the deceased, however, the Church merely uses the treasury to intercede on their behalf, *per modum suffragii*.

A Modern Debate

In the twentieth century, a debate arose concerning the efficacy of indulgences. In the account I have just presented, there is a neat split between indulgences offered for the dead and those for the living. While indulgences for the dead have a merely intercessory value, we can be sure that the indulgences received by the living are infallibly effective (within the aforementioned conditions). Some contemporary theologians, however, have argued that even indulgences received by the living possess a merely intercessory nature and that their efficacy is, consequently, indeterminate.

Bernhard Poschmann was one of the first to propose this theory. His historical research is invaluable and has served as a helpful resource for many in the attempt to better understand the origins of the practice of indulgences in the Church. Nevertheless, his historical knowledge prompted him to challenge the predominant theological understanding of indulgences. Poschmann placed great emphasis on the supposedly intercessory nature of the medieval absolution. As we saw, these absolutions were prayers offered by bishops on behalf of the faithful for the remission of temporal punishment before God. According to Poschmann, the contemporary indulgence, as the direct descendent of the absolution, also only has an intercessory value with respect to the effect before God.[50] As he explains:

> The efficacy of an indulgence rests primarily on the prayer of the Church which makes the remission of penance possible in the first place . . . remission of the pains of purgatory is besought from God, and depends on his gracious acceptation. Under this aspect an indulgence always operates *per modum suffragii*—and not only indulgences for the dead.[51]

If the Church was merely interceding then, so Poschmann suggests, then she is only interceding now.

According to his argument, the juridical nature of an indulgence only arose as a result of the attachment of the temporal effect, namely the

---

[50] Poschmann, *Penance and Anointing of the Sick*, 221.
[51] Poschmann, *Penance and Anointing of the Sick*, 231.

remission of the ecclesiastical penance.[52] This aspect of the concession was entirely within the jurisdictional authority of the Church and could be infallibly conferred by her decision. There was nothing wrong with doing this. In fact, it was wise and fitting. Nevertheless, the remission of temporal punishment before God remained a matter of intercession and suffrage. According to this argument, the "absolution" of *per modum absolutionis* referred exclusively to the juridical dispensation of the ecclesiastical penance.

With the course of time, however, the juridical nature of the remission of temporal punishment "spontaneously extended to the remission of the punishment of purgatory" in the minds of many theologians, according to Poschmann.[53] These theologians began to argue that the effect before God of the remission of temporal punishment was as certain and efficacious as the temporal effect. The theology of the treasury of satisfaction and of the legal authority of the Church to dispense of that treasury developed to justify this explanation. The indulgence, to put it simply, became entirely juridical. This change, so argues Poschmann, marks where the theology of indulgences went wrong. Whatever temporal effect was attached to an indulgence was certainly juridical, but the remission of temporal punishment has only ever been besought from God by means of the prayer of the Church, *per modum suffragii*. With respect to divine justice, all that the Church can do is intercede.

Needless to say, Poschmann's position was both influential and controversial. Karl Rahner, for example, defended the basic idea of Poschmann while slightly nuancing and altering the argument.[54] Rahner notes that critics of Poschmann could easily use his historical account to argue the opposite position. Why, in other words, is the primitive understanding of medieval absolutions determinative for the later theology of indulgences? Is it not possible that "the Church came to see only slowly in the course of all this, that her authoritative prayer has the efficaciousness of a jurisdictional enactment?"[55] The later development in theology could explain what had been happening from the beginning, even if the Church had not always possessed the means to articulate the nature and efficacy of her own action.

In order to defend Poschmann's claim, therefore, Rahner argues that it is not necessary to deny the juridical nature of an indulgence. The

---

[52] Poschmann, *Penance and Anointing of the Sick*, 215.

[53] Poschmann, *Penance and Anointing of the Sick*, 223.

[54] Karl Rahner, "Remarks on the Theology of Indulgences," in *Theological Investigations*, vol. 2, *Man in the Church*, trans. Karl-H. Kruger (London: Darton, Longman & Todd, 1963), 175–201.

[55] Rahner, "Theology of Indulgences," 187.

indeterminacy of an indulgence's effect can be maintained even if an indulgence remains a juridical act. He explains:

> If, however, this [payment] is to be taken as meaning that the Church does indeed (in certain circumstances) place her "Treasury"—in a jurisdictional act—completely at the disposal of the penitent by a plenary indulgence for the payment of the debt of temporal punishment due to sins but that it is an open question whether, and in what measure, God is prepared to accept this supplied payment in any particular case . . . then this is saying the same thing, in a more complicated terminology, as what Poschmann holds. For with regard to the end-effect, which consists in the effective payment of the debt of punishment, the jurisdictional process of placing the Treasury of the Church at the disposal of the faithful has exactly the same value as an intercessory prayer of the Church. Such a prayer is addressed to God in the form of an appeal to the merits of Christ and the Saints, i.e. the "Treasury of the Church."[56]

According to Rahner, an indulgence is a juridical act, authoritatively placing the treasury of the Church before God on behalf of the faithful. The Church does not merely intercede but offers satisfaction to God from the treasury entrusted to her. Nevertheless, the ultimate effect of this offering is determined by God alone. To put it simply, God is free to accept it or not.

Rahner's alteration is an improvement upon Poschmann's position insofar as it more accurately presents the situation of the Church. Poschmann cannot easily account for the distinct value of the intercession of the Church when he describes an indulgence simply as a prayer. Although the intercessory prayer of those entrusted with authority in the Church has a special efficacy, the unique power of the Church is more manifest when the treasury at her disposal is acknowledged. In the case of an indulgence, the Church does not stand before God empty-handed but presents to him what Christ and the saints have left her.

In addition, Rahner's account preserves the Thomistic thesis that an indulgence is not an outright forgiveness or dismissal of temporal punishment but a genuine payment. According to Rahner, the Church offers to God what is necessary to satisfy justice. Thus, even if Rahner argues that the acceptance of the payment is uncertain, his account better maintains this important point. As this doctrine of indulgences shows, even in God's

---

[56] Rahner, "Theology of Indulgences," 193.

gracious mercy the importance of justice and the need for satisfaction are still preserved.

That being said, Rahner is right to note that his position is not substantially different from that of Poschmann. His alterations avoid the principal difficulties, but if the effect of any indulgence is indeterminate, then the Church's authority is undermined. The Church not only has the authority to dispense of the treasury but, by the authority given her by God, also has the authority to *apply* that surplus to her children. Her authority is, therefore, twofold. It covers, in other words, not only her treasury but also the souls on earth. To say, however, that the Church can only intercede for her children denies that she truly possesses jurisdictional authority over them.

In the wake of the theological debate sparked by Poschmman and Rahner, Paul VI clarified this issue, confirming the traditional Thomistic doctrine. He writes, "In an indulgence in fact, the Church, making use of its power as minister of the Redemption of Christ, *not only prays but by an authoritative intervention dispenses* to the faithful suitably disposed the treasury of satisfaction which Christ and the saints won for the remission of temporal punishment."[57] Even more strikingly, the *Catechism of the Catholic Church* quotes the norms at the end of the aforementioned document, saying:

> An indulgence is a remission before God of the temporal punishment due to sins whose guilt has already been forgiven, which the faithful Christian who is duly disposed gains under certain prescribed conditions through the action of the Church which, as the minister of redemption, *dispenses and applies with authority* the treasury of the satisfactions of Christ and the saints.[58]

When an indulgence is granted to the living, therefore, the Church does not merely intercede for them as she does for the dead (*per modum suffragii*) but authoritatively applies the surplus satisfaction of her treasury to them (*per modum absolutionis*).

The Apostolic Pardon

Although not always referred to as such, the apostolic pardon imparted by a priest at the moment of death is simply a plenary indulgence. The *Manual of Indulgences* decrees, "A priest who administers the sacraments to someone

---

[57] Paul VI, *Indulgentiarum Doctrina*, 8 (emphasis mine).
[58] CCC, §1471 (emphasis mine).

in danger of death should not fail to impart the apostolic blessing to which a *plenary indulgence* is attached."[59] It is particularly fitting to receive this grace at the end of one's life in order to complete the necessary satisfaction for sin. As a juridical act like all other indulgences, its effect is certain and infallible. The one who receives it perfectly, therefore, retains no other obstacles to beatitude. Upon death, he would go immediately to heaven.

There is no better means at man's disposal for the remission of temporal punishment than the generous gift of an apostolic pardon. However, even if a priest is not able to be present at such a time, the Church still offers a plenary indulgence. The *Manual of Indulgences* explains, "If a priest is unavailable, Holy Mother Church benevolently grants to the Christian faithful, who are duly disposed, a *plenary indulgence* to be acquired at the point of death, provided they have been in the habit of reciting some prayers during their lifetime; in such a case, the Church supplies for the three conditions ordinarily required for a plenary indulgence."[60] So great is the generosity of God through the ministry of the Church that, by means of these concessions, none need leave this life with any remaining debt of temporal punishment.

Nevertheless, it is essential to reiterate a fundamental point we have seen throughout this book. The temporal punishment due to a sin cannot be remitted or satisfied if the sin itself has not been forgiven. Thus, the primary goal of any Christian at the moment of death should be to make a good act of contrition. True and fervent sorrow is needed to overcome the guilt of sin. The perfection of one's friendship with God is the most important. If someone dying received the apostolic pardon but was not truly sorry for all his sins—if he retained any attachment to sin—he would need to spend time in purgatory in order to complete his satisfaction before entering into the joy of heaven. Contrition, therefore, is of central importance. Importantly, but only secondarily, the person should seek to complete his satisfaction. When these two objects are sought in tandem, more than sufficient means are available for the complete restoration of man.

CONCLUSION

The doctrine of temporal satisfaction and indulgences thus presented confirms the claim at the beginning of the previous chapter: now is the acceptable time. There are so many graces and resources available during this life that it would be foolish to put off the work of satisfaction. Admittedly,

---

[59] *Manual of Indulgences*, Other Concessions, no. 12, §1.
[60] *Manual of Indulgences*, Other Concessions, no. 12, §1.

the debt of temporal punishment is not a question of salvation. All who die in a state of grace will eventually enjoy the beatific vision. However, a painful delay in purgatory awaits those who neglect the righteous demands of divine justice. How much better, therefore, to settle accounts now and to bear the just burden for wrongdoing. It will involve sacrifice, but the Lord is gentle.

As we have seen, in the pursuit of the reparation of divine justice man can even offer satisfaction for others and receive the satisfaction they offer for him. The greatest example of this exchange is when the Church applies the treasury of satisfaction left to her by Christ and the saints for the benefit of the faithful by means of indulgences. When she does, the Church not only remits the burden of temporal punishment but also encourages her children to grow in charity. As we have seen again and again, it is charity that is the most important.

When that charity truly takes root in the hearts of the faithful, the effect also redounds to a renewed zeal for satisfaction. As the witness of the saints proves, those who are most in love with God are also the most determined to make reparation to divine justice. When such holy souls earnestly take advantage of the means of satisfaction available to them, they can do more than enough to fulfill the debt of punishment. By the witness of these souls we ought to be reminded that the means to make complete and perfect satisfaction are at our disposal if we will but take advantage of them. Even in the last moment of life, the gift of a plenary indulgence is offered to all of the faithful who have been in the habit of reciting some prayers during their life. It cannot be repeated often enough: purgatory is not inevitable.

Conclusion

IN HIS ARTICLE ON THE doctrine of indulgences, Charles Journet speaks about the peculiar nature of writing about a theological topic of secondary importance. What he says can be applied to the present work as well:

> The truths of Christian doctrine are not all on the same level. They are arranged in a hierarchical order. It is identical to the case of the tree in which one distinguishes the roots, the trunk, the branches, the twigs [*fronde*]; or in the human body, in which one distinguishes the heart, the arteries, the capillaries. The doctrine of indulgences is similar to the fronds of a tree, to the capillaries of man. It is a secondary doctrine. It appeared at once in the course of the centuries in the West as the twigs of a vigorous and delicate tree. It could remain unknown for a long time, hidden. There was no risk in remaining this way. But it would be otherwise when, once manifested in its truth, it began to be voluntarily ignored, refuted, rejected. The drying out of the most periphery twigs of a tree, the malfunctioning of the capillaries is not disastrous in itself, but they concern the farmer and the doctor because they can be the hint of more hidden and ominous disorders.[1]

At least at face value, some may think that the doctrines presented in this book are not of central importance in the Christian life. Nevertheless, as we have seen, the theology at work touches on a number of important issues. It immediately connects us to notions of anthropology, sin, forgiveness, satisfaction, justice, punishment, virtue, transformation, and beatitude. As Journet suggests, error and confusion here can be a subtle sign of systemic issues. Thus, these secondary doctrines are not to be neglected.

According to the Thomistic account presented here, purgatory is the

---

[1] Journet, "Teologia delle Indulgenze," 4 (translation mine).

place where the souls of the just are purified after death of any remaining obstacles to their full enjoyment of divine communion. These include remaining venial sins, residual evil dispositions, and any debt of punishment which has not been completed through earthly penance. Venial sins are remitted in the first instant after death when the soul makes a perfect act of love in light of the penetrating illumination of the particular judgment. By the charity habitually present within it, the soul repents of all past sins. Forgiveness thus describes the perfection of man's relationship with God consequent upon the soul's actual reorientation to God through contrition. This point distinguishes Aquinas from Duns Scotus. Contra Scotus, forgiveness is not simply the endurance of a due punishment but involves a return of the will to God.

This movement of love, however, does not immediately rectify all of the soul's residual imperfections. At that moment the process of the soul's postmortem transformation is just beginning. Through repeated acts of charity providentially directed against the interior wounds of past sins, the soul is healed and restored to virtue. Divine light continues to pour into the soul as it painfully recalls and laments its failings. With each passing moment the soul is rectified as the remaining attachment to sin is slowly eroded. The soul reaches greater and greater perfection until it is finally prepared to behold the very face of God in heaven.

With such a perspective in mind, it is worth briefly revisiting the position of the Orthodox and Protestants seen in the second chapter. Although they have differences between them, in general, the Orthodox and Protestant descriptions of man's purification after death are not so different from the account I have just presented. Neal Judisch, as we saw, attempts to reconcile the Catholic and Protestant doctrines in this way. He explains that temporal punishment simply consists "in the individual's *enduring through* and *struggling to rectify* the *disorder of his soul* and *spiritual health* that sinful behavior brings in its wake."[2] Similarly, "'making satisfaction' for sins, in this context, is to be understood as the individual's *doing whatever is required* (and allowing God to do *to* him whatever's required) to *restore his spiritual well-being* and so to be *'purged' of his self-destructive attachment* to sin."[3] Despite the obvious material similarity, however, his position ultimately fails to distinguish adequately the analogous and multifaceted nature of punishment. "Temporal punishment" is certainly a broad category. In the widest sense, it can refer to all of the consequences of sin (excluding hell), but this extended notion

---

[2] Judisch, "Purpose of Purgatory," 176.
[3] Judisch, "Purpose of Purgatory," 176.

must include both the punishments from the order of reason and the punishments due to divine justice, as Aquinas distinguished them. The residual evil dispositions in need of healing are punishments of reason. Temporal punishment in a narrower sense, however, is a debt owed to divine justice. Even when we articulate a unified and harmonious integration of the two, they must remain conceptually distinct. The inadequacy of the Orthodox and Protestant doctrines of purgatory is not their description of the process per se but the theological categories they employ. They directly deny the satisfactory or retributive dimension of purgatory. In contrast, even when we describe the punishment of purgatory in medicinal and transformative terms, we must be able to identify and account for the indispensable punitive element. Any Catholic theology of purgatory must acknowledge the need for a personal share in satisfaction.

This claim is based on the nature of the restoration of the sinner in the Christian dispensation and the fundamental truth shown by Aquinas that disorder in a moral community must be addressed by an adequate punishment. It is a necessary part of the restoration of justice. This requirement is present within the universal horizon of divine justice as it is in the political community. When sufficient personal retribution before God is not accomplished by voluntary penance during one's life, it must be completed in purgatory. Aquinas teaches that such punishment traditionally includes the combination of the *poena damni* (temporary delay of the beatific vision) and the *poena sensus* (binding to material fire). Here, however, we can also incorporate the transformative illumination described above. Although Aquinas himself does not describe this aspect of purgatory, it is in fundamental accord with all of his principles. That being said, acknowledging a transformative element does not detract from the fundamental dynamic still at work. Justice in the universal community governed by God must be restored by the imposition of an adequate punishment. The wisdom and goodness of God is shown by the fact that this punishment is also medicinal.

Based on this description, it is best to say that the souls in purgatory endure a punitive healing, neither dimension of which should be neglected. By maintaining the undeniable importance of satisfaction and divine justice, this account accords with the heart of Catholic teaching about purgatory as discerned and expressed throughout the centuries. At the same time, it also incorporates the medicinal or transformative element which has been present at times within the tradition but has often struggled to find adequate theological expression.

It is worth mentioning the ecumenical potential of this point. Since the transformative dimension has been of primary concern to the Orthodox and Protestant explanations of purgatory, there is reason to hope that such a synthetic approach could bear meaningful ecumenical fruit. If the punitive and perfective dimensions of purgatory are united in a harmonious way that credibly incorporates genuine human transformation without abandoning the essential doctrinal core of the Catholic faith, the possibility of future reconciliation on this issue is brought somewhat closer.

Having thus considered the irreducible necessity of restoring the order of divine justice, it is important to recall by way of conclusion the abundant means at man's disposal for making satisfaction during this life. In addition to satisfactory works that flow from sacramental penance and a life marked by a spirit of repentance, man can also have recourse to the Church's generous dispensation of indulgences. By these juridical concessions the Church authoritatively applies to her children the superabundant satisfaction of Christ and the saints. If man is assiduous in seeking out these gifts, he can do much to eliminate the need for purgatory. The man who is thoroughly contrite for all of his sins and receives the Church's plenary indulgence at the moment of death assuredly goes immediately to heaven and avoids the painful purification of purgatory. Such should be the hope of us all.

Can the Souls in Purgatory Pray for Us?

IT IS WELL KNOWN THAT Aquinas denied that the souls in purgatory pray for those on earth, and many believe that this is the common teaching of the Church. In particular, Aquinas mentions his position in question eighty-three, article eleven of the *secunda secundae*, where he deals with the question of whether the saints in heaven pray for us. An objection asserts that because the souls in purgatory do not pray for us, neither do the souls in heaven. In response Aquinas writes, "Those who are in Purgatory, though they are above us on account of their impeccability, yet they are below us as to the pains which they suffer: and in this respect they are not in a condition to pray, but rather in a condition that requires us to pray for them."[1] In contrast, the saints in heaven, he thereby implies, are not suffering, and so are in the perfect condition to pray for us. Far from rejecting the premise of the objection, then, Aquinas merely explains why the fact that the souls in purgatory do not pray for us does not exclude the prayer of the saints in heaven.

The reason for the inability of the souls in purgatory to pray is explained in more detail in a preceding article of the same question. In article four, in response to an objection, Aquinas writes, "Those who are in this world or in Purgatory, do not yet enjoy the vision of the Word, so as to be able to know what we think or say. Wherefore we do not seek their assistance by praying to them, but ask it of the living by speaking to them."[2] To put it simply, we do not seek the intercession of the souls in purgatory because they have no way of hearing our petition. The saints who enjoy the beatific vision can know

---

[1] *ST* IIa-IIae, q. 83, a. 11, ad 3: "illi qui sunt in Purgatorio, etsi sint superiores nobis propter impeccabilitatem, sunt tamen inferiores quantum ad poenas quas patiuntur. Et secundum hoc non sunt in statu orandi, sed magis ut oretur pro eis."

[2] *ST* IIa-IIae, q. 83, a. 4, ad 3: "illi qui sunt in hoc mundo aut in Purgatorio, nondum fruuntur visione verbi, ut possint cognoscere ea quae nos cogitamus vel dicimus. Et ideo eorum suffragia non imploramus orando, sed a vivis petimus colloquendo."

man's thoughts through the knowledge that comes from their experience of God, but this kind of knowledge is ordinarily inaccessible to the souls in purgatory. Without knowledge of our situation, therefore, the souls in purgatory have no way to pray for our benefit. All that they can do is focus on the purification at hand.

That being said, some of the theologians we have seen in this book have challenged this Thomistic doctrine. Bellarmine and Suarez, in particular, both argued that the souls in purgatory do, in fact, pray for the souls on earth.[3] There has been no intervention of the Church to settle this issue, but I believe that the principles articulated in this book can help to identify the salient points to be considered and highlight a possible solution. As I will show, if the proper qualifications are kept in mind, it is reasonable to hold from a Thomistic perspective that the souls in purgatory do not ordinarily pray for those on earth but may occasionally be asked to do so as a part of their punitive healing.

As the second passage from Aquinas quoted above suggests, the first issue with the prayer of those in purgatory is the knowledge available to them. It is not difficult to imagine the will of the separated soul wishing good to a man on earth, provided he is able to have some knowledge of his situation. The principal challenge, therefore, regards the intellect.

In chapter four, we briefly saw that the separated soul operates according to an angelic form of knowledge, but in this context, we need to be more specific. The separated soul does retain the ideas acquired during its life on earth and preserved in its intellectual memory. These ideas form the essential foundation of the soul's cognitive activity after death. However, the extension of these ideas varies significantly between individuals and is hardly sufficient for all that is required for human thinking in this state. In his ordinary providence, therefore, God provides the separated soul with all the ideas necessary for its functioning. This providential dispensation is the divine illumination we saw above.

With respect to the prayer of the souls in purgatory, however, the problem of the knowledge of singulars (like particular people, for example) comes to the fore. In man's natural incarnate state, the ideas he forms through abstraction are universal. Thus, in order to think of singulars, he must make use of the imagination. Ordinarily, therefore, man does not have an intellectual knowledge of singulars, strictly speaking.[4] This thesis means, in consequence, that the ideas that man retains after death do not provide him

---

[3] Ott, *Fundamentals*, 323.

[4] *ST* Ia, q. 89, a. 4.

with knowledge of singulars. By means of its own ideas, in other words, the separated soul does not know individual people, not even those he "knew" on earth. Consequently, he cannot pray for them.

The fact that man cannot know singulars by means of his natural knowledge does not, however, mean that singulars are inherently unintelligible. God, who as pure spirit has no material imagination, knows all things, even singulars. Singulars, therefore, are not unintelligible in themselves. Rather, the key distinction is that singulars are unknowable by means of abstraction because that process necessarily excludes the matter which serves as the principle of individuation. It is, therefore, man's intellectual *process* that renders singulars unknowable to him in a direct way, and not the very nature of singulars themselves. From this distinction it follows that God can communicate knowledge of singulars to the separated soul in purgatory by means of infused species.[5] To put it simply, God can choose to share some of his own knowledge of particular individuals with the separated soul by means of a special illumination.

As I said above, this divine illumination is subject to the discretion of divine providence. God communicates those ideas that are necessary for the intellectual functioning of the soul. The separated soul, therefore, would certainly not know all singulars but only those that it ought to know. As Aquinas explains, "separated souls by these species know only those singulars to which they are determined by former knowledge in this life, or by some affection, or by natural aptitude, or by the disposition of the Divine order; because whatever is received into anything is conditioned according to the mode of the recipient."[6] We could imagine, for example, that someone might know his family and closest friends.

It is important in this context, however, to reconsider the initial concern of Aquinas presented in the first passage quoted above. Because of the unique state of these souls, suffering as they undergo their purification, they are ordinarily not in a condition to pray for us. The souls in purgatory are not simply idly waiting for heaven, thinking of whatever happens to occur to them. They are undergoing an intense period of purification that is directly guided by divine providence. We can imagine, therefore, that the ideas provided them in this state are directly related to the ways in which they need to be cleansed. In a similar way, the acts that God means to elicit by this

---

[5] *ST* Ia, q. 89, a. 4.

[6] *ST* Ia, q. 89, a. 4: "Animae vero separatae non possunt cognoscere per huiusmodi species nisi solum singularia illa ad quae quodammodo determinantur, vel per praecedentem cognitionem, vel per aliquam affectionem, vel per naturalem habitudinem, vel per divinam ordinationem, quia omne quod recipitur in aliquo, determinatur in eo secundum modum recipientis."

illumination are acts of love that include sorrow for past wrongs. There is no other finality to purgatory. It is exclusively aimed at accomplishing this process.

In this light, therefore, the concern of Aquinas makes more sense. The souls in purgatory do not pray for us not only because they do not typically know about our situation but also because they are intensely focused on God and their personal debt of justice. Every thought and act is specifically coordinated by God in order to bring this process to its fitting completion. Afterwards, as they enjoy the beatific vision in peace, they will more fully begin to cooperate with God's saving plan for his children and intercede on our behalf. In purgatory, however, they must remain wholly focused on their purification.

With this principle in mind, it is appropriate to say with Aquinas that the souls in purgatory do not ordinarily pray for those on earth. They typically do not know very much about us, and even if they could, they would ordinarily be entirely (and appropriately) absorbed in their own process of purification. That being said, it is not inconceivable that at times God might ask them to make intercession for a particular individual as a part of that process. There is nothing to prevent us from imagining that God communicates knowledge of the state of a given person to a soul in purgatory in order to bring about the needed charity and sorrow in his will. He might be asked, for example, to pray for those who are struggling with the same sins that he dealt with in life or perhaps for those whom he had wronged or injured in some way. If the example is not too trite, something of Ebenezer Scrooge's experience at the dinner table of his employee Bob Cratchit, even if somewhat fantastic, does not seem outside the realm of possibility for God's providential purification of the separated soul. Aquinas himself was well aware of the strong tradition that souls in purgatory occasionally appeared on earth to request the prayers of the living.[7] These examples suggest that God is not unwilling to be creative in the means he employs to bring about the necessary purgation. It is possible, therefore, that in a similar fashion, some souls in purgatory may occasionally be asked to repent of their sins by begging for the healing of someone still living. It is not hard, then, to further imagine that in his great mercy God would grant some grace to those still on earth in response to their prayers.

---

[7] *Super Sent.*, lib. 4, dist. 45, q. 1, a. 1, qc. 3.

Bibliography

Apostolic Penitentiary. *Manual of Indulgences: Norms and Grants*. Washington, DC: USCCB, 1999.

Aquinas, Thomas.[1] *Commentary on 1 Corinthians*. Translated by Fabian Larcher [paragraphs 987–1046 translated by Daniel Keating; Commentary of Peter Tarentaise translated by Beth Mortensen]. Edited and revised by the Aquinas Institute. Lander, WY: The Aquinas Institute, 2012.

———. *Commentary on the Gospel of Matthew*. Translated by Jeremy Holmes and Beth Mortensen. Edited by the Aquinas Institute. Lander, WY: The Aquinas Institute, 2013.

———. *Commentary on the Sentences of Peter Lombard: Book IV, Distinctions 1–13*. Translated by Beth Mortensen. Edited by the Aquinas Institute. Green Bay, WI: The Aquinas Institute, 2018.

———. *Compendium Theologiae*. In *Opuscula 1, Treatises*. Translated by Cyril Vollert. Edited and revised by the Aquinas Institute. Green Bay, Wisconsin: The Aquinas Institute, 2018.

———. *On Evil*. Edited by Brian Davies. Translated by Richard Regan. New York: Oxford University Press, 2003.

———. *Summa Contra Gentiles*. Books III–IV. Translated by Laurence Shapcote. Edited and revised by The Aquinas Institute. Green Bay, WI: The Aquinas Institute, 2018.

———. *Summa Theologiae*. Translated by Laurence Shapcote. Edited and revised by the Aquinas Institute. Green Bay, WI: The Aquinas Institute, 2018.

———. *Summa Theologica*. Translated by Fathers of the English Dominican Province. New York: Benziger Brothers, 1947.

---

[1] All Latin texts of Aquinas are taken from https://www.corpusthomisticum.org/ and were accessed from September 2019–July 2020.

"Articles of Religion." Anglicans Online. Accessed May 23, 2017. http://anglicansonline.org/basics/thirty-nine_articles.html.

Barnard, Justin D. "Purgatory and the Dilemma of Sanctification." *Faith and Philosophy* 24, no. 3 (July 2007): 311–30.

Bathrellos, Demetrios. "Love, Purification, and Forgiveness versus Justice, Punishment, and Satisfaction: The Debates on Purgatory and the Forgiveness of Sins at the Council of Ferrara-Florence." *The Journal of Theological Studies* 65, no. 1 (April 2014): 78–121.

Bellarmine, Robert. *De Controversiis: On Purgatory*. Translated by Ryan Grant. Post Falls, ID: Mediatrix Press, 2017.

Benedict XVI. Encyclical Letter *Spe Salvi*. November 30, 2007. Accessed March 24, 2023. https://www.vatican.va/content/benedict-xvi/en/encyclicals/documents/hf_ben-xvi_enc_20071130_spe-salvi.html.

Bentham, Jeremy. *An Introduction to the Principles of Morals and Legislation*. Edited by Jonathan Bennett. Early Modern Texts. 2017. Accessed March 7, 2020. https://www.earlymoderntexts.com/assets/pdfs/bentham1780.pdf.

Bouscaren, T. Lincoln, S.J., and Adam C., Ellis, S.J. *Canon Law: A Text and Commentary*. Milwaukee, WI: The Bruce Publishing Company, 1948.

Bracken, Jerry. "Thomas Aquinas and Anselm's Satisfaction Theory." *Angelicum* 62 (1985): 501–30.

Brown, David. "No Heaven without Purgatory." *Religious Studies* 21, no. 4 (December 1985): 447–56.

Callan, Charles J., O.P., and John A. McHugh. *Blessed Be God: A Complete Catholic Prayer Book*. Boonville, NY: Preserving Christian Publications, 2016.

Calvin, John. *Institutes of the Christian Religion*. Library of Christian Classics. Vols. 20–21. Philadelphia: The Westminster Press, 1960.

Cessario, Romanus. *The Godly Image: Christian Satisfaction in Aquinas*. Washington, DC: The Catholic University of America Press, 2020.

De Haan, David D., and Brandon Dahm. "Thomas Aquinas on Separated Souls as Incomplete Human Persons." *The Thomist* 83, no. 4 (2019): 589–637.

Denzinger, Heinrich. *Enchiridion symbolorum definitionum et declarationum de rebus fidei et morum: Compendium of Creeds, Definitions and Declarations on Matters of Faith and Morals*. Edited by Peter Hünermann, Robert Fastiggi, and Anne Englund Nash. 43rd ed. San Francisco: Ignatius Press, 2012.

Edwards, Jonathan. "Sermons and Discourses 1720–1723 (WJE Online Vol. 10)." Edited by Wilson H. Kimnach. Jonathan Edwards Center at Yale University.

Accessed January 11, 2020. http://edwards.yale.edu/archive/?path=aHR0c DovL2Vkd2FyZHMueWFsZS5lZHUvY2dpLWJpbi9uZXdwaGlsby9nZX RvYmplY3QucGw/Yy45OjQ6MDowOjU2LndqdZW8uODI4MDk4Ljgy ODEwMS44MjgxMDcuODI4MTEx.

Egan, M. F. "The Two Theories of Purgatory." *Irish Theological Quarterly* 17, no. 1 (1951): 24–34.

Fisichella, Rino. "Le indulgenze: definizione della problemática." Rome: Apostolic Penitentiary, 2015. Accessed April 3, 2010. http://www.penitenzieria.va/ content/dam/penitenzieriaapostolica/indulgenze/Fisichella.pdf

Fitzmyer, Joseph A. *The Gospel According to Luke (X–XXIV)*. The Anchor Bible Series. Garden City, NY: Doubleday & Company, Inc., 1985.

Garrigou-Lagrange, Réginald. *Life Everlasting and the Immensity of the Soul.* Translated by Patrick Cummins. Rockford, IL: Tan Books, 1991.

———. *Reality.* Translated by Patrick Cummins. Rockford, IL: Tan Books, 1991.

Gregory the Great. *Dialogues.* Edited by Roy Joseph Deferrari. Translated by Odo John Zimmerman. Fathers of the Church 39. Washington, DC: The Catholic University of America, 1959.

———. *Dialogorum Libri IV.* In Patrologia Latina 77. Edited by J. P. Migne. Paris: Petit-Moutrouge, 1849.

Guevin, Benedict M. "Anselm and Aquinas on Satisfaction." *Angelicum* 87 (2010): 283–90.

Hütter, Reinhard. "Human Sexuality in a Fallen World: An Economy of Mercy and Grace." *Nova et Vetera* 15, no. 2 (2017): 433–64.

John Paul II. General Audience of September 29, 1999. Accessed March 9, 2020. http://www.vatican.va/content/john-paul-ii/en/audiences/1999/documents/ hf_jp-ii_aud_29091999.html.

Journet, Charles. "Théologie des indulgences." *Nova et Vetera* 41, no 2 (1966): 81–111. Italian: "Teologia delle Indulgenze." Accessed April–July, 2020. https://it.scribd.com/document/33798703/Ch-Journet-Teologia-delle-indulgenze.

Judisch, Neal. "Sanctification, Satisfaction, and the Purpose of Purgatory." *Faith and Philosophy* 26, no. 2 (April 2009): 167–85.

Jugie, Martin. *Purgatory and the Means to Avoid It.* Cork, Ireland: Mercier Press, 1949.

Koritansky, Peter. *Thomas Aquinas and the Philosophy of Punishment.* Washington, DC: The Catholic University of America Press, 2011.

Lewis, C. S. *Letters to Malcom: Chiefly on Prayer*. London: Geoffrey Bles, 1964.

Louismet, Savinien. *Mysticism—True and False*. 2nd ed. London: Burns & Oates Ltd.. 1919.

Luther, Martin. *Large Catechism*. In *Book of Concord*. Translated by Theodore G. Tappert. Philadelphia: Muhlenberg Press, 1959.

Lutheran-Catholic Dialogue. *The Hope of Eternal Life*. Washington, DC: USCCB, 2010. Accessed August 25, 2021, https://www.usccb.org/committees/ecumenical-interreligious-affairs/hope-eternal-life.

Maritain, Jacques. *St. Thomas and the Problem of Evil*. Milwaukee: Marquette University Press, 1942.

Mark Eugenicus. "Marci Archiepiscopi Ephesii Oratio Prima de Igne Purgatorio." In *Documents Relatifs au Concile de Florence*, 39–60. Vol. 15 of Patrologia Orientalis, edited and translated by Louis Petit. Turnhout: Editions Brepols, 1990.

———. "Marci Archiepiscopi Ephesii Oratio Altera de Igne Purgatorio." In *Documents Relatifs au Concile de Florence*, 108–151. Vol. 15 of Patrologia Orientalis, edited and translated by Louis Petit. Turnhout: Editions Brepols, 1990.

McCarter, P. Kyle, Jr. *II Samuel*. Anchor Bible Series. Garden City, NY: Doubleday & Company, Inc., 1984.

McIlmail, Edward. "Indulgence Clarification: Total Detachment from Sin." November 18, 2010. Accessed July 17, 2020. https://spiritualdirection.com/2010/11/18/what-is-total-detachment-from-sin-more-indulgence-clarification.

Melanchthon, Philip. *Apology of the Augsburg Confession*. In *Book of Concord*. Translated by Theodore G. Tappert. Philadelphia: Muhlenberg Press, 1959.

Michel, A. "Purgatoire." *Dictionnaire de Théologie Catholique*. Paris: Libraire Letouzey et Ané, 1936.

Milgrom, Jacob. *Numbers*. JPS Torah Commentary Series. Philadelphia: The Jewish Publication Society, 1989.

Moorman, Mary C. *Indulgences: Luther, Catholicism, and the Imputation of Merit*. Steubenville, OH: Emmaus Academic, 2017.

Mother Mary of St. Austin. *The Divine Crucible of Purgatory*. Revised and edited by Nicholas Ryan. Newport News, VA: Providence Foundation, 1940.

Nietzsche, Friedrich. *The Genealogy of Morals.* Translated by Horace B. Samuel. London: T.N. Foulis, 1913. Accessed March 7, 2020. https://www.gutenberg.org/files/52319/52319-h/52319-h.htm.

O'Brien, John Joseph. "The Remission of Venial Sin." STD diss., Catholic University of America, 1959.

O'Neill, Colman E. *Meeting Christ in the Sacraments.* Rev. ed. by Romanus Cessario. New York: Alba House, 1991.

Ott, Ludwig. *Fundamentals of Catholic Dogma.* Translated by Patrick Lynch. Edited by James Canon Bastible. Charlotte, NC: Tan Books, 1974.

Paul VI. Apostolic Constitution *Indulgentiarum Doctrina.* January 1, 1967. Published in Apostolic Penitentiary. *Manual of Indulgences: Norms and Grants.* Washington DC: USCCB, 1999.

Poschmann, Bernhard. *Penance and Anointing of the Sick.* Translated by Francis Courtney. Eugene, OR: Wipf and Stock Publishers, 1964.

Rahner, Karl. "Remarks on the Theology of Indulgences." In *Theological Investigations.* Vol. 2, *Man in the Church,* 175–201. Translated by Karl-H. Kruger. London: Darton, Longman & Todd. 1963.

Suarez, Francisco. "De Purgatorio." In *Opera Omnia.* Vol. 22. Paris: Apud Ludovicum Vives, 1861.

Scotus, John Duns. *Ordinatio Liber Quartis: A Distinctione Decima Quarta ad Quadragesimam Secundam.* In *Opera Omnia.* Vol. 13. Vatican City: Typis Vaticanis, 2011.

Spezzano, Daria. "'Be Imitators of God' (Eph 5:1): Aquinas on Charity and Satisfaction." *Nova et Vetera* 15, no. 2 (2017): 615–51.

Van Roo, William A. *Grace and Original Justice According to St. Thomas.* Analecta Gregoriana 75. Rome: Apud Aedes Universitatis Gregorianae, 1955.

Vander Laan, David. "The Sanctification Argument for Purgatory." *Faith and Philosophy* 24, no. 3 (July 2007): 331–39.

Vanhoutte Kristof K. P., and Benjamin McCraw, ed. *Purgatory: Philosophical Dimensions.* Cham, Switzerland: Palgrave Macmillan, 2017.

Ware, Kallistos. "'One Body in Christ': Death and the Communion of Saints." *Sobernost (Incorporating Eastern Churches Review)* 3, no. 2 (1981): 179–91.

Walls, Jerry L. *Heaven, Hell, and Purgatory: Rethinking the Things That Matter Most.* Grand Rapids, MI: Brazos Press, 2015.

———. *Purgatory: The Logic of Total Transformation.* New York: Oxford University Press, 2012.

Index